Jamaica

Jamaica

Text by Jack Altman
Revised by Lindsay Bennett, Robert Kerr
Photography: Pete Bennett
Cover photograph by Pete Bennett
Photo Editor: Naomi Zinn
Layout: Media Content Marketing, Inc.
Cartography by Raffaelle Degennaro
Managing Editor: Tony Halliday

Fifth Edition 2002
Revised 2003

Contacting the Editors

Every effort has been made to provide accurate information in this publication, but changes are inevitable. The publisher cannot be responsible for any resulting loss, inconvenience or injury. We would appreciate it if readers would call our attention to any errors or outdated information by contacting Berlitz Publishing, PO Box 7910, London SE1 1WE, England. Fax: (44) 20 7403 0290;
e-mail: berlitz@apaguide.co.uk www.berlitzpublishing.com

Printed in Singapore by Insight Print Services (Pte) Ltd, 38 Joo Koon Road, Singapore 628990. Tel: (65) 6865-1600. Fax: (65) 6861-6438

060/305 REV

CONTENTS

- A ☛ in the text denotes a highly recommended sight

Jamaica

SEA WEEDNG F205
990/167

JAMAICA AND ITS PEOPLE

The island of Jamaica will be near the top of the list for anyone planning an idyllic holiday getaway. With warm sunshine, beautiful beaches, lush tropical scenery, and fine hotels, it is guaranteed to provide a little rest and relaxation. However, with a vibrant grassroots culture and the growing confidence of an independent nation, it defies the advertising stereotype of the "deserted island." Jamaica is not just a destination—it is an experience.

The third-largest island in the Caribbean, just south of Cuba, Jamaica is 233 km (145 miles) in length and 83 km (52 miles) across at its widest point. The island is aligned almost east-to-west in the water so that sunrise wakes the eastern tip, proceeds to caress the length of the island, and kisses the western tip "good night." Geographically it is extremely diverse, with a central backbone of high mountains and hills blanketed with a mixture of wet limestone forests and plantations of pine and native hardwood trees, such as mahoe and cedar. These are surrounded by areas of limestone formations, scrub and grassland, coral cliffs, and fine sand beaches. Fresh water from tropical storms feeds 120 rivers and some of the most celebrated waterfalls and cascades on earth.

On land, there is a wealth of animal and bird life. Rare species of butterflies and delicate hummingbirds take to the air, and crocodiles and manatees still live in and around vast tracts of mangrove swamp in the south. The island is surrounded by coral reefs and reef walls, which provide shelter to sea creatures and recreation to divers and snorkelers.

Temperatures here vary only a few degrees from about 27°C (80°F), although the heat is tempered by the nearly continuous

Schoolchildren in uniform are a common sight on the streets in the capital city of Kingston.

trade winds that blow across the Atlantic. In the mountains and hills of the interior, the temperature drops with altitude to as low as 3°C (37°F) on the mist-covered Blue Mountain Peak, the highest point on the island.

Much of the land is extremely fertile and produces a range of tropical fruit and vegetable crops, providing ample food for the people and such lucrative cash crops as sugar and coffee. Four hundred years ago these crops brought British colonists to rule the land and African slaves to work it. The bitter taste of slavery is always in the background.

Today's Jamaican population is a mixture of African and English, with Spanish, Indian, and a smattering of Portuguese Jews, Chinese, Welsh, and Irish. They have been melded together, giving rise to a fascinating national "identity." Since independence in 1962, the black majority has worked to create a country based on confidence from within, working on a principle of pride in oneself and in one's roots. This is so important for the future of the country that the national motto is "Out of many—one people."

It says much about the character of the Jamaican people that they have slightly changed the story of Columbus and his trip to the island in 1493. He is not held in the same high esteem here as he is in other islands. As someone has said, Columbus only thought that he had discovered Jamaica. In actuality, it was the population of Jamaica who discovered *him*—Columbus was really lost, thinking that he had found another route to Asia.

Vestiges of the British colonial legacy can still be found, not least in the fact that English is Jamaica's official language: the popularity of cricket is another example. The thirteen regional parishes and numerous towns were originally named after British settlements. You can find Manchester, Sheffield, and Cambridge in Jamaica, to name but three. However, these British influences have, even from the earliest days of colonial rule, always been tempered and molded to the Jamaican style. Jamaica has always had a second, "unofficial" language developed from the early days of slavery. This creole, a mixture of English, African, and Spanish words and phrases, is still evolving and often indecipherable to the outsider. Next to town names derived from England, you'll also find names such as "Wait Awhile" and "Fruitful Vale," derived from the land and lifestyle of Jamaica. And as for cricket, Caribbean players have turned the tables on their colonial mentors and the island has produced some of the best players in the world, capable of outplaying the Brits.

By the late 20th century the influence of the United States was much stronger than that of Britain. Many Jamaicans head to the States for further education, and the American economic influence on areas such as business investment and planning is growing. It's no surprise that the US dollar is accepted as readily as the Jamaican dollar to pay for goods.

But Jamaica is not simply turning blindly into a small version of its bigger brother. It still revels in its own identity, which is now internationally recognized through such influential cultural products as the Rastafarian religion and reggae music. The followers of Rastafarianism (with their characteristic mane of "dreadlocks") originated in Jamaica in the 1930s and are still predominantly found here. Jamaican music—ska and, especially, reggae—has, since the 1970s, been exported and enjoyed around the world. The strong beat and earthy lyrics seem to symbolize and celebrate the character of this young and lively country.

Jamaicans are sociable, living their lives out in the open and knowing everything about their neighbor's business. There's nothing they like better than having a good chat

Rastafarianism

One of the most popular images of Jamaica is that of the Rastafarian. His mane of dreadlocks and colorful "tam" hat are instantly recognized worldwide. Rastafarians live by a series of strict rules. They are nonviolent and do not eat meat. Rastas use marijuana as an integral part of their religious experience and do not cut their hair, fearing the same loss of spiritual and physical strength that the biblical Samson experienced.

Members of the Rastafarian sect believe themselves to be one of the tribes of Israel, viewing the modern world as "Babylon," synonymous with evil, and they seek peace with God, whom they believe is in all beings. Their spiritual leader is Haile Selassie, the late emperor of Ethiopia; who was God's messenger on earth—the "Lion of Judah."

about the latest bit of gossip: who is doing what, where, and why. They are very direct in their dealings with each other, as you might discover if you come across a friendly conversation among a group of friends. The loud, raucous Jamaican English dialect and the waving hands reflect the joy with which social relations are conducted here. They are equally direct in their dealings with visitors, too, so don't expect a shy Jamaican smile as you walk by. Instead, be prepared for a barrage of questions about your life, offers to supply anything you need, a host of jokes at your expense, and some *serious* flirting. Jamaicans can definitely be "in your face." But don't feel intimidated, as the attitude is not personal. Having some lines ready to throw back can often induce guffaws of laughter and an appreciative slap on the back.

Examples of Rastafarian culture are on display—and for sale—at this shop in Negril.

The recreational pleasures that some islanders enjoy have become synonymous with the name Jamaica: dancing to the heavily rhythmic musical beat; taking a little marijuana (or "ganja," as it's known here), which many Jamaicans view as a medicinal herb; or simply sitting back and chatting with friends on a bench or street corner, where the situation is described as "Irie"—the equivalent of "Everything's just fine!"

Jamaican youths paint a fishing boat on one of the island's beautiful beaches.

Jamaicans appear to worry little about the future; sometimes it seems that they don't worry about what happens in the next few minutes. The popular phrase "Soon come" indicates an apparent lack of concern about time and an unhurried attitude to daily tasks, but this is a misconception. Occasional hurricanes can spoil the idyllic climate and contribute to this "laid back" attitude, forcing people to be accept that circumstances can suddenly alter dramatically and yet life carries on. To have to wait a while for something is not the worst problem in the world.

Since independence in 1962, tourism has been Jamaica's primary industry and the island has become renowned as one of the prime destinations in the Caribbean. The best beaches

The "Meet the People" Program

This outreach effort has been established by the Jamaican Tourist Board to provide visitors with a chance to discover how ordinary Jamaicans live. The families involved, almost one thousand of them, open their homes to visitors. If you have a special interest, the tourist board will match you with an individual or family with similar passions. This is an excellent way to experience the everyday lives and culture of your hosts.

have become home to the finest hotels, aiming to supply everything needed for the perfect vacation. All-inclusive packages and large resort hotels offer restaurants, sporting activities, entertainment, wide-screen sports TV channels in the bars, shopping, and sunshine. There is a temptation never to tear oneself away from the hotel. Yet to do this is to miss the very essence of what the island is all about. Step out of the hotel and your senses will be bombarded by a range of sights, sounds, smells, tastes, and textures that let you know that you could only be in Jamaica.

Such sights include the colorful "ites", green and gold "tams" (red, green and gold knitted hats, worn by Rastafarians, to cover their mane of dreadlocks); the red *ackee* fruit on the tree. Sample *ackee* cooked with saltfish, Jamaica's national dish, and the smell of hot jerk pork cooked in a pit barbecue. Hear the modern-day dance hall and reggae music booming from a hundred cranked-up car stereos or the chorus of frogs that begin to call as evening descends. Feel the texture of a hand offered in greeting and try to fathom the "Jamaican handshake," a ritual whose rules seem to be more complex than those of the game of cricket.

The traditional Jamaican handshake—with clenched fists meeting first vertically then horizontally, after which the thumbs touch briefly—signals a parting of mutual understanding and respect.

Of course Jamaica has its palm-lined beaches and almost endless rum drinks, and you can enjoy a wonderful resort-based break. But once you begin to look underneath this initial veneer of a "do-nothing-in-the-tropics" holiday, it's like peeling the layers of an onion. There's an abundance of nature, history, art, and modern culture to be explored and enjoyed. Jamaica is an island with a strong personality that doesn't simply wait in the wings. It comes out to meet you.

A BRIEF HISTORY

The earliest signs of people on Jamaica are the remains of the Taino, Amerindians who were the descendants of Arawak-speaking people. Historians disagree over the meaning of the name Taino, some claim that it means "peace" while others suggest its meaning is more akin to "men of good". Whatever the exact translation of the name, the Tainos were a peace-loving people who migrated from the north coast of South America. They traveled to various Caribbean islands along the entire Antillean chain, arriving in Jamaica at the beginning of the eighth century. The Tainos left an important legacy of rock paintings and carvings in places such as Runaway Caves near Discovery Bay, and shards of pottery found at their settlements near Nueva Sevilla and Spanish Town have added a little to our knowledge about them. Over 200 Taino sites have been identified, and it is said that when the Spanish arrived in Jamaica there were approximately 100,000 Tainos living on the island. They called Jamaica *Xaymaca* ("land of wood and water").

Columbus and the Arrival of Europeans

Columbus first arrived in Jamaica on 5 May 1494 at Discovery Bay, where there is now a small park in his honor. He stayed for only a few days but returned in 1502, landing here when the ships of his fleet became unserviceable; he waited at St. Ann's Bay for help to arrive from Cuba. After the death of Columbus in 1505, Jamaica became the property of his son Diego, who dispatched Don Juan de Esquivel to the island as Governor.

Esquivel arrived in 1510 and created a base called Nueva Sevilla near St. Ann's Bay, from which he hoped to colonize the rest of the island. The Spanish immediately began

Historical Landmarks

c. 700 Arawak-speaking Amerindians arrive on Jamaica from the Orinoco region of South America.

1494 Christopher Columbus lands on the north coast of Jamaica, claiming it for Spain.

1502 Columbus is stranded for several months near St. Ann's following damage to his ships.

1510 First Spanish settlement founded at Nueva Sevilla.

1517 First boat carrying African slaves arrives on the island.

1655 British forces take the island from the Spanish. The Spanish free their slaves, who head to the interior of the island.

1670 The Treaty of Madrid cedes Jamaica to England.

1692 A powerful earthquake destroys the city of Port Royal.

1739 Peace treaty with freed slaves (Maroons), which offers them self-government.

1700s The number of African slaves increases dramatically, with around 250,000 working on Jamaican plantations.

1838 Emancipation of enslaved people.

1865 Morant Bay rebellion seeks better conditions for the liberated slaves.

1938 Difficult economic conditions lead to the formation of the first trade unions and political parties.

1944 Universal adult suffrage is introduced.

1962 Jamaica declares independence led by the JLP.

1972 Victory at the elections for Michael Manley and PNP.

1976 Landslide electoral victory for PNP.

1980 The JLP returns to power, led by Edward Seaga.

1989 The PNP, led by Michael Manley, win the elections.

1993 P. J. Patterson of the PNP becomes Prime Minister.

1997 Michael Manley dies. The PNP return for a third term.

2002 The PNP win an unprecedented fourth term.

A statue of Christopher Columbus at St. Ann's Bay recalls Spanish occupation.

subjugating the Arawak population, many of whom died under the yoke of oppression and of diseases carried by the Europeans. A number of them committed suicide rather than live the life created for them by the Spanish.

The site of Nueva Sevilla proved to be unhealthy and mosquito-ridden, and in 1534 the Spanish founded Villa de la Vega, today known as Spanish Town. Pig breeding was the main occupation of these early settlers, but they also planted sugar cane and other crops that required large numbers of laborers. The number of Taino had already fallen dramatically, so the Spanish began to import enslaved people from Africa to work the land; the first Africans arrived in 1517.

The opportunities that the island had to offer were never really exploited by the Spanish. They were much more interested in the gold and other treasures to be found in South America. However, they had to protect the shipping lanes in order to get their treasure home, and this meant keeping hold of as much of the Caribbean (or the "Spanish Main," as it was then known) as possible. They fortified the more strategic islands, but Jamaica was deemed less important than Cuba or Puerto Rico and, consequently, was poorly protected.

British Rule

In 1654 Oliver Cromwell, Lord Protector of England, dispatched a British fleet to the Caribbean to break the stranglehold of the Spanish. They were repulsed at Hispaniola by a strong Spanish force and decided to take Jamaica as a consolation prize. They sailed into what is now Kingston Bay in May 1655 and sent an ultimatum to the capital. The small Spanish force considered its position and decided to retreat, heading to the north coast and sailing to Cuba. Before they left, they freed their slaves, who fled into the interior of the island.

The Spanish attempted to retake the island in 1658 at the Battle of Rio Bueno but were defeated; however, this did not alleviate Jamaica's problems. Other European powers began to put pressure on the defending forces, and British naval power in the area was badly stretched. Sir Thomas Modyford, the Governor of Jamaica, offered a deal to pirate ships already well established in the area: if the pirates protected British assets, then they were free to harass enemy shipping with impunity. They agreed; Modyford issued letters of

The Lady Pirates

The fierce pirates who sailed the Caribbean were joined by two women, Mary Read and Anne Bonney, who were said to be as ruthless as their compatriots. They dressed in men's clothing and committed unspeakable atrocities in the name of profit. Captured by the British authorities, they were found guilty of piracy and sentenced to death, but both pleaded "the belly." Judges would not kill an unborn child, so both sentences were commuted to life in jail. Mary Read and her young child died of fever only a few months later, but there is no record of what happened to Anne Bonney. Her life after the trial is a mystery.

accreditation which authorized the pirates to act in the name of the British Crown.

These "privateers" were welcomed at Port Royal, the English settlement on the southern tip of Kingston harbor, and it quickly developed a reputation as the wickedest city in the world. Plunder was now legitimate business and the city was awash with money and booty from the numerous pirate raids. There was little evidence of religion or of the rule of law. Henry Morgan was chief among the pirate leaders. He and his followers conducted a successful series of bloody raids on Spanish settlements in the Caribbean, culminating in the sacking of Panama, the major city of the Spanish Main.

In 1670 the Spanish officially ceded Jamaica to British rule as part of the Treaty of Madrid, and the British began a systematic process of settlement, offering land and aid to prospective settlers. They rescinded their agreement with the privateers

From pirate to policeman—a portrait of Captain Henry Morgan in Port Royal.

and began the process of evicting them from Port Royal. Henry Morgan was offered the post of Lieutenant Governor of the island and charged with driving out his former cohorts. The erstwhile pirate thus became a policeman during the last years of his life. Morgan died in 1688 before his task was complete, but nature finished what he had started: Jamaica suffered a powerful earthquake in 1692, and Port Royal sank into the sea, taking with it many of the treasures stolen from the Spanish. The surviving pirates took to the sea once again.

Plantations and Slavery

As the 18th century began, the British colony of Jamaica was putting the disaster at Port Royal behind it. The trade in sugar cane and spices was becoming profitable. However, there was a problem. Plantation work was labor intensive, but there were very few laborers on the island; the Spanish slaves had disappeared into the inhospitable interior and the native Tainos had been decimated by disease. The decision was made to import a work force from West Africa, resulting in some 600,000 slaves being transported to Jamaica over the next few decades. One in five slaves died en route, and many more died of disease once on the island. However, there seemed to be an inexhaustible supply sailing across the Atlantic. On the back of this cruel system, Jamaica gradually became the biggest sugar producer in the world and a very wealthy island indeed.

The colony slowly became better organized. Thirteen administrative parishes were created, forming the basis of government that we still see today. The Governor, official voice of the monarch, commissioned a representative (or custos) in each parish. Powerful land-owning families organized an Assembly to run the everyday affairs of the island, but many landowners continued to live in Britain, where they exerted tremendous influence in Parliament. They ensured that the interests of

Jamaica, or at least their own interests on the island, were always at the forefront of decisions made in London.

However, even in these early days there were slaves who fought against the tyranny of the system. The original slaves whom the Spanish had released after 1655 became known as "Maroons," from the Spanish word *cimarrón* (which means "wild" or "untamed"). They made their settlements in the hills away from British rule but began to attack colonists in a program of raids now remembered as The First Maroon War. British forces suffered constant harassment at their hands and even named a part of the island "The Land of Look Behind" in recognition of the surprise attacks they suffered. Eventually the British began to force the Maroons into more isolated and remote pockets of land.

This war of attrition ended in 1739, when agreement was reached between the two sides. The Maroons were allowed self-rule in certain designated areas in return for not inciting or helping the plantation slaves. This agreement is at the root of Maroon self-government today. The slaves themselves also began organizing revolts (the first in 1760), but their situation remained the same. Treatment of slaves was for the most part cruel and inhumane, with family life virtually destroyed as fathers were systematically split from mothers and their children.

During the American War of Independence, Jamaica came

Built in the 1650s and rebuilt after the earthquake of 1692, Fort Charles protected Jamaica for some 250 years.

under threat again from other European powers, which saw Britain's problem to the north as a chance to capture its colonies in the Caribbean. Some islands were taken by the French, but Admiral Rodney saved Jamaica by defeating the French fleet at the Battle of Les Saintes in 1782. Jamaica thereafter became an island of strategic importance for the British, who based a large naval fleet at Fort Charles in Port Royal.

Emancipation

The French Revolution in 1789 sent ripples of discontent through the Caribbean. The French peasants' cry for freedom prompted another Maroon War on Jamaica, after which many

Maroons were deported to Nova Scotia. There was, however, a growing movement against slavery in Britain. In 1807 Parliament made the trade in slaves illegal, but the powerful sugar lobby exerted pressure and slavery continued on the plantations. The slaves were angry and dispirited, but nonconformist churches broke the monopoly of the Church of England and encouraged the slaves to stand up and take action against injustice. This intervention guaranteed the popularity of these Christian denominations; today, you will find Baptist and Adventist churches in almost every settlement, their congregations still as strong today as in the early 1800s.

The momentum for change was growing, and in 1831 a black lay preacher named "Daddy" Sam Sharpe led a revolt of 20,000 slaves at Montego Bay. After a campaign of great destruction, the authorities assured them that slavery would be abolished. Sharpe and approximately 1000 other slaves surrendered peacefully, only to be rounded up and publicly executed. This news was met with revulsion in Britain, and moves to liberate the slaves culminated in full freedom in 1838. Many retreated into the hills to make their own way, the forefathers of today's small-scale, self-sufficient farmers.

Unfortunately, being "free" solved none of the problems suffered by the population. There was no economic infrastructure outside the plantation system, and power remained in the hands of a small minority of white and mixed-race individuals. Meanwhile, Asian laborers took up the work previously carried out by the slaves; their descendants can still be found on the island, particularly around Little London in the west. As a further blow to the economy, the British Parliament passed the Sugar Equalization Act in 1846 as part of a new free-trade policy. Jamaica's protected market was effectively gone.

In October 1865 at Morant Bay, there was another uprising, led by Baptist minister Paul Bogle and by George Gordon, a mulatto (mixed-race) landowner. It brought savage retribution from the authorities, and both leaders were executed. But it prompted the dissolution of the Jamaica Assembly, which was dominated by plantation owners. The island became a Crown Colony ruled directly from London, and over the next few years there were several reforms to its political and social systems.

Island of Bananas— banana production hastened the tourist trade in the late 19th century.

As the sugar trade declined in importance, economic disaster loomed. Fortuitously, another crop found favor with the industrial world: Jamaica became the island of bananas. The first consignments were exported in 1866 and, within a few years, thousands of tons were being shipped to markets in the US and Britain. The boats carrying the banana crops also fostered the beginnings of the tourist trade. The first visitors arrived as passengers on them, spending time around Port Antonio. Charmed by the tropical paradise, word quickly spread about the beauty of Jamaica.

Still there was little change in conditions for the black majority, who had no economic or political power. The world-wide depression of the 1930s brought a new wave of demonstrations in Jamaica, and a number of individuals emerged to lead the people and pave the way for nationhood. Marcus Garvey called for black self-reliance, and Alexander Bustamante formed the Industrial Trade Union and later the Jamaica Labour Party

In its heyday Port Antonio was known as the undisputed "banana capital of the world."

(JLP). The Jamaica Trades Union Congress and the National Workers Union allied themselves to the People's National Party (PNP), led by Norman Manley in opposition to Bustamante. Together, these organizations fought for local rule, which in 1944 resulted in universal voting rights for adults.

At the same time, the early years of World War II brought American tourists who were no longer able to travel to Europe on holiday. Jamaica's popularity as a tourist destination was now undeniable.

Independence and Democratic Rule

In the postwar period there continued to be constitutional changes, including self-government for Jamaica in 1959. Britain hoped to create a Federation of Caribbean Islands in the region. But the Jamaicans voted instead for full independence, which became official on 6 August 1962. Jamaica is also a nation within the British Commonwealth.

Since independence the political culture of Jamaica, which started out with such confidence and optimism, has been fraught with problems. Violence and corruption have been constant factors in the political process.

From 1962 until 1972, the JLP held power. The party's broad aims were to support capitalist policies and to continue close ties with Britain and the rest of the Commonwealth. In 1972, however, the left-wing PNP was elected with a massive majority but with little change in the economic power of the people. Michael Manley, son of Norman, led the party and pushed for policies that brought Jamaica closer to independent nonaligned countries. Manley was criticised for political links to Fidel Castro's Cuba, foreign investment dried up, wealthy Jamaicans left the island, and the economy declined. The uncertain and volatile situation led to gang violence, and Jamaica seemed to be heading for civil war. In 1980 the JLP returned to power following a campaign that saw the deaths of several hundred people. The JLP leader, Edward Seaga, reintroduced capitalist policies and foreign investment began to trickle back.

Challenges Ahead

In 1989 the PNP regained power, governing under the leadership of Percival Patterson since 1993. There are plans to use the cultural wealth of the island to create a real national identity. But the problem of economic and social inequality remains, and violence, which accompanies political allegiance, remains a part of everyday life in the ghettos of Kingston.

Notwithstanding its status as a member of the British Commonwealth, Jamaica looks toward the US for its future. Its proximity to the US—only 90 minutes from Miami by air—means that cultural influences for the young are found in American entertainment media and sports. Jamaica seeks to combine these influences with its own strong identity to create an independent and stable society.

Famous and Important Jamaicans

Samuel Sharpe *(1801–1832)* Sam Sharpe, a literate slave and a lay preacher, encouraged his congregation to lay down their tools until their grievances had been addressed. The resulting protest started peacefully at Christmas, but turned violent. It was brutally suppressed, and Sharpe was executed on the Parade in Kingston. However, the sympathetic reaction of the British public to his fate resulted in eventual emancipation for Jamaican slaves. Memorialized in Sam Sharpe Square in the center of Montego Bay's downtown area, he is one of Jamaica's "National Heroes."

Sir Alexander Bustamante *(1884–1977)* Born William Alexander Clarke, Bustamante was appalled by social conditions in Jamaica, he began working for social equality, forming the Bustamante Industrial Trade Union, only to be imprisoned in 1938. In 1944 he worked with the British to negotiate the island's independence; he subsequently formed the Jamaica Labour Party (JLP) for the first election under the new adult suffrage rules. The JLP won; he became Jamaica's first Prime Minister after independence. He retired from politics in 1967 and was named a "National Hero."

Marcus Garvey *(1887–1940)* Born in St. Ann's Bay, Garvey was a printer who, after leading an unsuccessful strike in 1914, was exiled from Jamaica. He later founded the Universal Negro Improvement Association, which called all those of African descent in the colonies to unite and break their reliance on white people. After founding an office in Harlem, New York City, he returned to Jamaica to continue his work but was imprisoned for fraud on what are now considered false charges. He died in London but is now buried in Jamaica, another of the island's "National Heroes."

Bob Marley *(1945–1981)* Marley was the pioneering musician who brought reggae out of the ghettos of Jamaica and presented it to a world audience. He was also a Rastafarian, and his adherence to the codes of this faith encouraged a new interest in the fledgling religion. Throughout his life he campaigned against poverty, oppression, and the political violence that was paralyzing his homeland. One of the major influences on Jamaican youth culture, he died of brain cancer at a very young age, but his legacy lives on throughout the world in his music. You can visit his mausoleum in the town of Nine Mile as well as the Bob Marley Museum in Kingston.

WHERE TO GO

The island of Jamaica offers a wealth of activities, sites, and attractions. Many visitors choose to remain in a single resort area and enjoy the creature comforts of beach, restaurant, and nightclub. Others are eager to explore nature's wildlife at the bottom of a coral reef or at the top of a mountain peak. Wherever you go in Jamaica—from the tropical coasts to the rugged interior to the secluded eastern tip of the island—you'll find fascinating people and landscapes. In this chapter, we journey clockwise around the island, starting at Montego Bay on the northwest coast. Along the way, you're sure to discover places you never knew existed in Jamaica, worth an hour's visit or several days of exploration.

MONTEGO BAY, OCHO RIOS, AND THE NORTH COAST

The northern coast has been the major focus of tourist development on Jamaica since the 1970s. Much of the new development has occurred here, and in some places this has changed the character of the landscape. However, there's no denying that this area has just about everything needed for a perfect holiday, whether you want to do nothing but sit on a beach, dive and snorkel along the coral reefs, enjoy sports, or explore the history and culture of the island.

Montego Bay

"MoBay" (as it's called by the locals) is probably the most complete resort area in Jamaica, with its beaches, sports, and shopping along with a large number of fine hotel resorts. It is almost nonstop fun, and because it is only minutes from the international airport, there is no lengthy transfer to your hotel. The town is also surrounded by a host of different attractions.

Sunset across Montego Bay—a moment of tranquility in the otherwise action-packed center of tourism.

Its disadvantage, if it matters, is a lack of attractiveness: it is a rather soulless hodgepodge of development with no real character. But if you are here simply to have fun, you might not even notice.

This tourist heartland is also home to 100,000 Jamaicans who live in the hills surrounding the town. Originally named Villa Manteca by the Spanish ("Fat City," because they used to butcher wild pigs in the area), Montego Bay developed into a center for sugar cane and became a banana port under colonial rule. During World War II, the US built an Air Force base here that later became the international airport. This and the harbor, which attracts modern cruise ships, guaranteed Montego Bay a large slice of Jamaica's tourist action.

Downtown

The resort sits on the east side of the wide bay, with the cruise port on the west. **Downtown Montego Bay** is located between the two. It is a jumble of loud and boisterous streets, full of people, dogs, and goats breathing the fumes of hundreds of buses and cars. Thousands of makeshift shacks sell beer or cigarettes, and hundreds of oil-barrel barbecues cook jerk chicken and burgers. Roads meet at **Sam Sharpe Square**, originally Charles Square but renamed after the hero of the 1831 slave rebellion who was hung for his part in the uprising. In one corner of the square are the **Cage**, an old prison lockup built in 1806 to house drunken sailors or runaway slaves, and the **Ring**, the site of the once-regular slave auction. However, this isn't the place to be after dark.

Nearby, **Fustic Street Craft Market** is a constant buzz of activity. This is the place to come to check out the full range of local handicrafts and souvenirs. The windows and doors of over 100 wooden cabins are bedecked with printed sarongs, T-shirts, and carved masks. Try your hand at haggling and you are guaranteed to get a better price than you thought.

In Jamaica the car horn is always used when overtaking vehicles and pedestrians. When driving you should adopt the same practice. Sound it also on blind curves. Jamaicans expect to hear horns and will respond to them—so should you.

Just on the outskirts of downtown are a couple of shopping malls that carry international duty-free goods. The Montego Bay Shopping Centre is air-conditioned and under cover, but the newer Bay West Centre has the added attraction of well-known fast food outlets—for that little touch of home.

Beaches and Resorts

Head east to the **Gloucester Avenue** "strip" for the beaches and resort life. This is the place to be for all the action, with some of the busiest bars, loudest music, and wildest water sports on the island. As you reach Gloucester Avenue, you'll pass the remains of the **Old Fort**, with its small sturdy walls and heavy cannon that guarded the bay for many years.

Most beaches in MoBay are private, which means you pay a small fee to enter. They are kept neat and tidy, with water-sports facilities and areas for changing and showering. The first one along the strip is **Walter Fletcher Beach**, which on weekends is popular with the town dwellers of Montego Bay. The beach is home to **Aquasol Theme Park**, which offers loads of family fun and sports activities by day and has open-air dining and a disco in the evening.

Farther along the strip is **Doctor's Cave Beach**, the original Montego Bay beach developed in the Edwardian era when sea bathing became a popular pastime throughout the British Empire. It became a center for wealthy and upper-class visitors and was donated to the town in 1906 by the original owner. It is still as popular as ever and the sand is sublime, but the cave after which the beach was originally named was destroyed in the early 1930s during a hurricane. **Cornwall Beach**, another private beach with perfect sand and sheltered waters, can be found behind the **Jamaica Tourist Office** building, a short distance east along Gloucester Avenue.

West of the Bay

The cruise port, or **Montego Bay Freeport**, sits on an outcrop on the west side of the bay. It is a popular stop on cruise itineraries. There is a small shopping center on site, but the main duty-free malls and the beaches are only minutes away.

This area is also home to the **Montego Bay Yacht Club**, which hosts a number of yachting regattas through the year. You can hire boats here to take a morning or full day out at sea for sport fishing or just a relaxing jaunt.

A little way off the coast is **Montego Bay Marine Park**, established in 1992. The park has 26 sq km (10 sq miles) of reef, sea-grass, and mangrove swamps and covers an area west of the town to the site of Montego Bay airport. A number of companies offer underwater tours in glass-bottomed boats or submersible craft, or you can rent snorkel or scuba gear to get a closer look yourself. These can be booked from the offices at **Pier 1**, a small marina with cafés and shops that sits in the middle of the bay between the beaches and the cruise port.

Walter Fletcher Beach—popular on the weekends among the town dwellers of Montego Bay.

South of the Bay

South of Montego Bay there are a number of attractions that make enjoyable excursions, if you want to tear yourself away from the beach or book an outing from your cruise ship.

The Barnett Estate, with its 18th-century great house, has been owned by the Kerr-Jarrett family for over 250 years. Their ancestor Nicholas Jarrett arrived on the island in 1655, and the family was at the forefront of economic and political activities on Jamaica for many generations. They once owned almost all the land on which Montego Bay now stands. You'll be able to tour the still-operating plantation and wander around the great house, which has been restored with many original touches.

Near the town of Anchovy, **Rocklands Bird Sanctuary** offers a fascinating close-up encounter with the birds of Jamaica. The sanctuary began almost by accident in the late 1950s when founder Lisa Salmon moved onto a plot of land high in the hills above Montego Bay. She loved the hummingbirds that inhabited the garden and began to befriend them so that they came regularly for feeding. Now you, too, can come eye-to-eye with these beautiful tropical birds; the sanctuary provides sugar water and seed so that you can feed them. The buzzing sound of the wings signals their approach and, if you are lucky, they will fly up and perch on your finger to take the food.

Switch to Jamaican time. The phrase "Soon come" means that things will happen eventually. Don't be in a hurry for anything.

High in the hills 27 km (17 miles) south of Montego Bay is **Belvedere Estate**. It is a working plantation producing a mixed crop of spices and fruits, but it also opens a fascinating window on plantation life during colonial times. The current

Yachts and sailboats moored at Montego Bay—a mix of private vessels and charter crafts available for day trips.

owners have created an agricultural museum to demonstrate the traditional methods of crop production as well as everyday life on the plantation. The staff wear traditional clothing and work with the tools of their forefathers. You'll even be able to consult a traditional herbalist to cure your ailments. Swimming pools and a restaurant add a modern dimension to the trip.

East on the Coast Road

East along the main coast road from the Montego Bay area, there is a string of luxurious resort hotels with facilities like golf courses and equestrian centers. Two shopping malls at Ironshore and Half Moon Resort have duty-free shopping and fast food outlets. A number of sightseeing attractions lie along this route, which leads to Falmouth and, eventually, to Ocho Rios.

Greenwood Great House, once home to one of the wealthiest and most powerful colonial families on the island.

Rose Hall Great House is, perhaps, the most infamous house in the whole of Jamaica. Set high on a hill above the coast with commanding views, it was built by John Palmer in the late 18th century and named after his wife Rose. It later became the home of Annie Palmer when she married into the family; it is Annie who has given the house its fame and reputation. She was a woman who struck fear into the heart of the local population. They said that she was a white witch with potent magical powers who had murdered three husbands and an unidentified number of lovers before she herself died under mysterious circumstances. Locals, who believed that the house was haunted by her spirit, buried her nearby so that she could be reunited with her body and rest in peace.

The house fell into ruin after emancipation, when fear of the witch's influence drove the plantation's slaves away. In 1966 it was bought by the Rollins family, who began the difficult and time-consuming job of totally renovating the building. Rich mahogany wood cut from trees from the surrounding estate has been used to great effect in the refurbished house where new floors and ceilings had to be built. The interior has been redecorated with fabrics and furniture dating from the late 1700s to Victorian times. The ballroom has a woven wall-covering that is a reproduction of an original by Philipe de la Salle, which he created for Marie Antoinette. Be sure to experience the beautiful views from Annie Palmer's upstairs sitting room, where you can see along the coast and catch a cooling sea breeze. Here, it is said, she plotted the death of her husbands and lovers.

Farther east, **Greenwood Great House** was once the property of one of the wealthiest and most powerful colonial families in Jamaica. The first Barrett family member came to Jamaica with the invading English forces. His descendants were major landowners from the middle of the 16th century and played an important role throughout the colonial history of Jamaica, holding positions of great influence in the judiciary and administrative bodies. Another (and perhaps more famous) member of the family was Elizabeth Barrett, who

Jamaica Highlights

Near Montego Bay *Belvedere Estate* (on the B8 road, tel: 956-7310), open daily 10am–4pm. *Bob Marley Mausoleum* (Nine Mile), open daily 8:30am–5pm. *Greenwood Great House* (on the A1 road, tel: 953-1077), open daily 9am–5pm. *Martha Brae Rafting* (Falmouth, tel: 952-0889, 940-6398), open daily 9am–4pm. *Nuevo Seville* (St. Ann's Bay, tel: 972-2191), open daily 9am–5pm. *Rocklands Feeding Station* (on the Anchovy Road, tel: 952-2009), open daily 2pm–5pm (3:30pm regular afternoon feeding time). Rose Hall Great House (on the A1 road, tel: 953-2323), open daily 9am–6pm. Runaway Caves, (tel: 973-2841), open daily 9am–5pm.

married poet Robert Browning. She was born in England but never came to the island: the responsibility for working the plantation lands fell to her male relatives.

This house, begun in 1780, was only one of the Barrett properties in the area and was built for entertaining rather than for use as a home (the main Barrett residence, Cinnamon Hill, is now owned by the singer Johnny Cash). It is now home to the Bettin family, who are custodians of its treasures. The house has many original features and authentic touches. Furniture and art collected over the generations fills the house, but perhaps most fascinating is the collection of original musical instruments and machines used for entertainment before the advent of electricity. A fine Scandinavian piano, a polyphone machine with disks, and a pianola were all used for dancing or recitals in the ballroom. The library is the largest of any plantation in Jamaica, with over 300 volumes, including three first editions; the books would have been used to while away the long humid days. In 1826 Richard Barrett won £800 in a competition when the house's entryway was selected as the best mile of macadam road in Jamaica. The approach to the house must have been truly spectacular at that time, but today you must drive with a little care, as its condition is a bit rough.

Just before the town of Falmouth is **Charles Swaby's Jamaica Safari Village**, home of the Jamaican crocodile and other tropical creatures. This wetland area covers a vast amount of mangrove swamp and has been turned into a nature theme park. You can travel by boat into the very heart of the swamp to get a close-up look at the secretive creatures. Scenes from the James Bond film *Live and Let Die* were filmed here.

Falmouth

Once an important port for the shipment of molasses and sugar, **Falmouth** has many buildings dating from the early 1800s. But despite its colonial heritage, most visit Falmouth because it is the center for **rafting** on the **Martha Brae River**. It is one of the most popular activities on Jamaica (see page 88). The river is 48 km (30 miles) long, and the 1½-hour raft ride covers 5 km (3 miles) of navigable river that meanders through the lush countryside, where you can take in the verdant river banks and the peace and quiet. It's a cool and relaxing way to be pushed along, almost like a tropical gondola ride. Each raft is hand-built by the raft captains to carry two adults. The rafts are made of bamboo from the surrounding countryside and can be used for only four months before they have to be replaced.

Just to the east of town is a small scruffy bay that comes to life at night. Called by several names (including "Glistening Waters"

Riding on bamboo rafts along the Martha Brae River is a relaxing way to enjoy the lush countryside of Falmouth.

Discovery Bay's Columbus Park houses a number of eclectic exhibits that celebrate Jamaica's history.

and "Luminous Lagoon"), it is officially known as **Oyster Bay**. Once darkness falls, the water in the bay is filled with luminescent micro-organisms that glow when agitated. It is almost as if someone has immersed a neon light in the water. You can take an evening cruise to watch this fascinating phenomenon and dip a hand in the water to make it happen yourself.

From Cockpit Country to St. Ann's Bay

In the highlands and hinterlands south of Falmouth is **Cockpit Country**, an amazing and almost impenetrable landscape of limestone plateau (or "karst") pitted with holes and fissures that have created fantastic formations. Deep depressions and high outcrops are blanketed by layers of green vegetation and topped by a lush canopy of trees, making travel difficult and at times dangerous. It is here that the Maroon people chose to live after they had been freed by their Spanish owners in 1655.

Even today there are few roads—this really is one of the last true vestiges of wilderness in Jamaica. Because much of the area is inhospitable to human activity, it is a lush area for birdlife and rare plant species that have disappeared from other parts of the island. You can find hundreds of caves in the limestone fissures, and some intrepid visitors go "spelunking," exploring their watery interiors. If you want to see the area or investigate the caves, do take a guide and go well prepared.

Scattered Maroon villages remain, their inhabitants still making a meager living out of the poor soil. Tours of the village of **Accompong** and the Native Arawak cave drawings nearby can be arranged through the Jamaica Tourist Board. One of the best times to visit is in early January, when the Maroon people hold a major festival.

Farther east along the coast lies **Discovery Bay**, said to be the place where Columbus landed in 1494 on his second journey from Spain. The precise location is still disputed, as some say that he landed farther along the coastline. Nevertheless, a small park on the roadside at Discovery Bay stands as a tribute to his achievement. **Columbus Park** is built on land donated by the Kaiser Bauxite Company, whose industrial site now dominates the bay. The Park includes an

Duppies and Obeah

Most Jamaicans believe in the powers of magic and the underworld. Periods of bad luck or ill health are often seen as evidence of black-magic spells put on individuals. "Duppies" are spirits of the dead who come back to earth. Good or evil, they can be manipulated by those still alive for mischief or revenge; "obeah" is the local term for this type of sorcery. Look for colored paint around the windows of homes, intended to prevent spirits from entering.

eclectic collection of objects from the history of Jamaica: old railway memorabilia, artifacts from sugar cane processing plants, and a banana-tallying machine can all be found here.

Just outside Discovery Bay are **Runaway Caves**, which are easily accessible and safe to explore. The system stretches up to 16 km (10 miles) inland and includes Green Grotto, a vast cavern with an underground lake where stalactites are clearly reflected in the glassy water. Arawak paintings, though fading, can still be seen on the walls of the caves. Guided tours are well organized and include a boat trip on the lake.

The main polo season in Jamaica sees match after match on the pristine grass at **Chukka Cove**. For those who like other horse-riding activities, there is also an equestrian center that organizes exhilarating rides on the beach and trips along guided trails through the surrounding hills.

Runaway Bay is the appropriately named area of coastline where slaves were said to have escaped the island to try to find a better life; often they traveled the 145 km (90 miles) to Cuba. Today Runaway Bay is one of the most popular resorts on the northern coast. A series of hotel complexes has sprung up to take advantage of the fine beaches. The diving and snorkeling opportunities along the reef wall here are said to be the best in Jamaica. Most hotels offer instruction and organized dives out to **Ricky's Reef** or the **Canyon**, two major reef areas. There are also a couple of small aircraft lying offshore (relics of drug runners who ran out of luck) that make fascinating artificial dive sites.

In the hills south of Runaway Bay is the village of **Nine Mile**. This is where the singer and social commentator Bob Marley was born and spent the early part of his life. The village is tiny and a total contrast to the bustle of the Trenchtown ghetto in Kingston, where he lived as a recording superstar. Marley's body was brought here after his death and lies in a mausoleum, where he is buried with his prized guitar. The surrounding land and the tree under which he sat as a child have been turned into a shrine to the singer, but the ambiance is spoiled by the numerous "guides" and souvenir sellers who crowd your path to the entrance. Inside the compound you'll find genuine Rastafarian guides. The whole site is painted in the bright green, red, and yellow colors that represent nature, blood, and sunshine. The **Bob Marley Mausoleum** lies in a small church with other symbols of Rastafarian faith, including a photograph of Haile Selassie (their spiritual leader) and the lion of Judah depicted on a stained glass window.

To the east is **St. Ann's Bay**, birthplace of the black activist Marcus Garvey. His statue can be found on Main Street, outside the town library. It is also the site of **Sevilla la Nueva**, the original Spanish settlement on Jamaica, founded in 1509, which sits just to the west of the modern town. Columbus is said to have landed here in 1503 when his fleet was in a desperate state of repair. Two of his ships were abandoned in the harbor but, despite many attempts by archaeologists to locate them, they have never been found. Columbus spent some months at an Arawak settlement here before assistance arrived and he made his way back to Europe.

A Bob Marley statue in Kingston pays tribute to Jamaica's famous son.

A fishing boat rests in the shade on the riverbank near Ocho Rios.

The Spanish settlers built a sugar factory here in 1515 and attempted to develop the site, but the persistent fevers contracted from mosquitoes in the swamps forced them to move and create a new capital at Spanish Town in 1538. However, Sevilla la Nueva was not completely abandoned, continuing as a working plantation and rum distillery that were later developed and expanded under British rule. The most obvious remains at the site date from this time. There are vestiges of the rum distillery, cattle pens, and a large pimento barbecue for roasting allspice berries. Older remains lie scattered along the shoreline and in shallow water beyond the tidal reach. Many areas are being actively excavated and look a little ramshackle. A small museum in the English great house displays finds from the site.

Ocho Rios

Jamaica's second tourist town is a relatively recent creation. **Ocho Rios** began in the 1960s when the site of a fishing village was systematically developed with the express aim of turning it into a resort. There are several large hotel complexes here, and the town is a popular destination for cruise companies, with several ships calling at the port each week.

Ocho Rios is Spanish for "eight rivers," but this name is not descriptive of the area. It is thought that the town was named following an English mistranslation of the Spanish phrase *las chorreros*, meaning "river rapids," as there are a number of these near the town. There is very little left of old Ocho Rios: the scant remains of **Ocho Rios Fort** are probably the oldest and now lie in an industrial area, almost forgotten as the tide of progress has swept over the town.

Jamaica's Best Beaches

Long Bay (Negril). Seven miles of fine, golden sand gently sloping into shallow water. Low-rise development leaves room for hundreds of palm trees.
Booby Cay (Negril). Lying just off Long Bay, this tiny island provides sand all around its rocky interior.
Doctor's Cave (Montego Bay). The original tourist beach and still as popular as ever, with lots of activities. Come and be sociable.
Lime Cay (Port Royal). Just think "Robinson Crusoe" and you'll have the right idea. But avoid weekends, when it's more like "Grand Central Station."
Turtle Beach (Ocho Rios). Everything is in one place, and you get a great view of cruise ships arriving and departing.
Frenchman's Cove (Port Antonio). Fine white sand in sheltered coves, with lots of tropical vegetation. Wander through the coral outcrops to find a private corner.
Long Bay (eastern tip). Just the place for long romantic walks, as rolling Atlantic waves break on miles of pink sand. Not suitable for swimming because of dangerous undertow.
Holland Bay (eastern tip). Fine white sand and not another soul in sight.
Treasure Beach (south coast). With numerous fishing boats, this dark volcanic sand beach is not just for tourists.

The main waterfront area, **Turtle Beach**, sits in front of the town center. It is a wide arc of sand, shallow and sheltered. You must pay a small fee to enter, but the sand is kept clean and there are facilities and refreshments available. You'll be able to hire a boat to take you out to the reef that runs all along the coast here, easily seen just a few hundred meters from the shore; snorkeling offers the opportunity to observe a wealth of fish and other sea creatures. Jamaica's largest hotel, the Radisson Renaissance Grande Hotel, overlooks Turtle Beach.

The main activity in the town is shopping. In fact, Ocho Rios is a virtual shopping mall for the cruise passengers who arrive in the hundreds on most days of the week. There are a number of expensive jewelry and other duty-free shops, all with goods priced in US dollars (duty-free goods must always be paid for in foreign currency). It's a veritable treasure-trove of quality gems, gold, and cigars. Take a look around the incongruous pink Taj Mahal shopping mall or Soni's in the center of town. The latter complex, with over 100 shops, probably has the widest choice. There is also a thriving craft market behind the main beach,

Jamaica Highlights

Near Ocho Rios *Blue Lagoon* (off the A4 road at Fairy Hill, tel: 993-8491), open daily from 9:30am. *White River Valley,* (St. Mary, tel: 974-2017), open daily 9am–5pm. *Brimmer Hall* (southwest of Port Maria), open daily. Tours at 11am, 1:30pm, and 3:30pm. *Dunn's River Falls* (on the A3 road, tel: 974-2857), open daily 8am–5pm. *Firefly* (Oracabessa, tel: 997-7201), open daily 8:30am–5:30pm. *Nonsuch Caves* (southeast of Port Antonio, tel: 993-3740), open daily 9am–5pm. *Prospect Plantation* (on the A3 road, tel: 994-1058), open daily. Tours Mon–Sat 10:30am, 2pm, and 3:30pm; Sun at 11am, 1:30pm, and 3pm. *Rio Grande Rafting* (Berridale, tel: 993-2871), open daily 9am–5pm.

A jitney tour takes tourists around Prospect Plantation to see crops of coffee, sugar, bananas, and plantains.

where you will be able to haggle for locally produced goods, from a T-shirt to a necklace of semiprecious stones. Once the business day stops, there are few bars and restaurants in the town; evening activity tends to focus on the large hotels.

Ocho Rios, though not the prettiest town on the island, has a number of advantages as a destination choice. It has beautiful natural attractions nearby, and it makes a good base for other, longer journeys around Jamaica, being within relatively easy reach of Kingston, the Blue Mountains, and the coast road that leads to both Montego Bay and Port Antonio.

Dunn's River Falls

If you visit only one place on Jamaica outside your hotel, then this should be it: a place of fantastic natural beauty and flowing water that epitomizes the Arawak name for Jamaica, *Xaymaca*

Giant cottonwood trees draw visitors to scenic Fern Gully south of Ocho Rios.

("land of wood and water"). Only 5 km (3 miles) west of Ocho Rios, **Dunn's River Falls** is a series of limestone cascades that carry the water of Dunn's River almost to the sea. The cascades fill with clear water and are surrounded by overhanging vegetation. Modern tradition demands that you climb up through the bubbling cascades as part of a human chain. Lines of people, all holding hands, do a slightly wobbly "conga" to the top, where everyone forgets decorum and gets very wet in the pools. It's fun and totally tropical, but you'll be very lucky if you have the pools to yourself to enjoy the kind of romantic experience advertised in the tourist brochures.

Guides are optional, but they are sure-footed and will take care of your camera until you reach the top. Don't forget to take a change of clothing and a towel. There are wooden walkways at the side of the falls for those who don't want to get quite so wet.

Gardens, Rivers, and Plantations

The road leading south from Ocho Rios climbs out of the town and twists and turns through a narrow valley of tropical vegetation called **Fern Gully**. Five km (3 miles) of giant cottonwood trees, with their tangle of thick roots, frame varieties of giant fern to create a canopy of fronds and leafy branches over the road. Insects, frogs, and birds call together in a cacophony of sound. It feels so humid in the midst of the vegetation—with sunlight streaming through the upper branches and steam rising from the damp ground—that you can imagine being on the set of a prehistoric dinosaur film.

Ocho Rios is surrounded by not only areas of natural beauty but also by landscaped tropical splendor. There are three gardens in the area, all admired among gardening connoisseurs and all with different specialties to explore. Choose one, or visit all three to get a comprehensive overview of tropical environments, not to mention some pointers for caring for house-plants that can be purchased back home. The first is **Coyaba River Garden and Museum**. *Coyaba* is the Arawak word for "paradise," and this garden, set high above Ocho Rios, lives up to its name. Plants, trees, and native birds are complemented by rivers and streams teaming with fish and turtles. The small museum at the site traces the history of the island from the time of the Arawak.

Set on the hillside above the town, **Shaw Park Gardens** has wonderful views; it comprises 14 hectares (35 acres) of tropical plants and natural waterfalls that once formed the grounds of the now closed Shaw Park Hotel.

Twenty minutes drive from Ocho Rios, in the parish of St Mary, is one of the area's undiscovered nature attractions, **White River Valley**. This nature retreat and fun spot has tubing, horseback riding, biking and hiking along forest trails and the chance to sample a sumptuous Jamaican meal.

The **White River** runs east from Ocho Rios and marks the boundary between St. Mary Parish and St. Ann Parish. **River rafting** takes place here, and although the journey is not as long as at Martha Brae (see page 37), it is possible to enjoy a swim at a natural pool as part of the trip, so bring along some swimwear. You can also enjoy an evening river cruise, when the banks are lit with torches. Turn off the main road just before the White River Bridge to find the Calypso rafting base.

On the main coast road east out of Ocho Rios is **Prospect Plantation**, which offers tours by jitney and horse trails through crops of coffee, bananas, plantains, and sugar cane. The well-informed guides will give you plenty of information about the natural and introduced flora of the island. The Spanish settled the land and grew crops here in the 17th century, but the fine "great house" was built by English colonists in the 18th century. The plantation was bought in 1936 by English industrialist Sir Harold Mitchell and became an important focus for diplomatic, political, and social activities in Jamaica. Many important dignitaries have visited the house, and it has become a tradition for trees to be planted to mark each special occasion. The tour passes trees planted by the Royal family of Luxembourg, Andrew Young, and the Duke of Edinburgh, among many others. You can also plant your own tree at the plantation, which can grow next to those planted by the "great and good." The plantation also houses a private academy for young people, the brainchild of Harold Mitchell. It promotes the ideal of good citizenship through hard work and community service. Many former academy students have gone on to high rank in the diplomatic and civil services.

A little farther east is **Harmony Hall**, a beautiful Methodist minister's residence built in 1886. The house, which has been home to an art gallery since 1981, has been elegantly preserved with pretty painted wood fretwork and stained shutters. The gallery on the upper floor has a collection of some the best art and crafts in Jamaica. Original paintings from local and guest artists, ceramics, and a collection of imported crafts make it a good place to find a souvenir of high quality. Beneath the gallery is an Italian

Fishing boats on White River near Ocho Rios. Rafting trips and evening cruises are popular pastimes on the river.

restaurant. During the season there are many exhibitions and performances in the gardens of the hall; ask at the Tourist Board office for information.

Firefly and Annotto Bay

The coastal road continues east through the small town of **Oracabessa**, with its decaying iron fretwork, and on to **Galina Point**, the most northerly part of Jamaica. Set high on a bluff overlooking the coastline at Galina Point is **Firefly**, the former home of Noel Coward, dean of British theater and cinema and the archetypal Englishman. Coward had the house built in 1956 and lived here until his death, creating a haven where he could be out of the public eye. The house is surprisingly small and simple, with one bedroom, a tiny kitchen, and a couple of social rooms. What makes it special is its position, with magnificent views of the coastline east toward Port Antonio and southeast to the peaks of the Blue Mountain range. The song "A Room with a View," which Coward wrote in 1928, inspired him to build the house on this spot.

The parties Coward held here were legendary. Film stars such as Elizabeth Taylor, Sophia Loren, and Charlie Chaplin were entertained with songs at the grand pianos that still sit in the main room. Coward valued his private life, however, and guests were never allowed to stay overnight at Firefly. In fact, there was no room for them. They were given guest quarters at Blue Harbour, another house farther down the hill that Coward also owned; it can clearly be seen from Firefly's garden.

Coward died in 1973 and is buried in the garden, at his favorite spot overlooking the coastline. His simple gravestone is decorated daily with a small vase of fresh flowers. A short video presentation in the old garage gives a fascinating background to the man and his prodigious talent.

Also on the grounds is a small, sturdy building, much older than Coward's house. In the 17th century, pirate Henry Morgan and his band of cut-throats used the building to plan their dastardly deeds. With tiny windows and thick walls, it made a perfect secret hideaway for counting stolen "pieces of eight."

Nearby is the house of another famous person, an author whose fictitious main character has taken on an almost-real persona. **Goldeneye** was home to Ian Fleming when he wrote all the "James Bond" novels. Fleming came to Jamaica in 1942 while serving in British Intelligence, decided to settle here, and bought the house in 1946. Although Bond was noted for his bravery and prowess, he was in fact named after a man of very different talents: Fleming took the name of his "007" hero from the author of the book *Birds of the West Indies*, which had been researched and written a few years earlier. For people with deep pockets, the house is now available to rent.

Inland from Firefly is **Brimmer Hall Plantation**, a working plantation of 809 hectares (2,000 acres) that produces a variety of crops including bananas, coconuts, and citrus fruit. It has a beautiful great house, made (unusually) of wood and filled with an eclectic collection of furniture from the colonies of the British Empire. The tour, by jitney, shows how the plantation works, with knowledgeable staff to answer questions and give demonstrations of such skills as the correct technique for climbing banana trees.

The main road continues to hug the north coast, but just before reaching Annotto Bay there is a turn south in the direction of Kingston. Take this route to reach **Castleton Botanical Gardens** some 18 km (11 miles) inland. The 37 hectares (91 acres) of garden are set on lands above the Wag Wag River, which twists through a steep and narrow valley. They were landscaped in 1862 with a large consignment of plants from Kew Gardens in London. Exotic plants from every corner of the British Empire were subsequently brought here before being transplanted to other gardens on the island. It might not be the oldest, but Castleton is regarded by many as the "father" of tropical gardens in Jamaica because of its work in the propagation and distribution of new plant genera.

PORT ANTONIO AND THE BLUE MOUNTAINS

The eastern area of Jamaica is the most tropical and (according to many) most beautiful part of the island. The high peaks of the Blue Mountains dominate the landscape. This is where swathes of lush virgin rainforest mix with plantations of coffee on the high mountain slopes and meet thousands of verdant banana plants that blanket the coastal plains. The mountains attract moisture sweeping across the Atlantic Ocean and are thus often swathed in heavy rain clouds that feed the forests and fill numerous streams and rivers. There are few major roads in this area. The main route follows the coastline, circumventing the mountains and leading to some of the least-visited areas of Jamaica that are totally off the tourist track.

The western approach to Port Antonio is characterized by huge groves of banana plants, which in earlier times made the town one of the richest in the Caribbean. All along the northern coast here you will see remains of the old railway line, which once linked the plantations to the port but now mostly provides a place for children to play or animals to graze. The station houses, however, still give an impression of the grandeur of the recent past. The line was closed in 1985, but with the speed at which the native plants have reclaimed the land, it might have been a hundred years ago.

Port Antonio

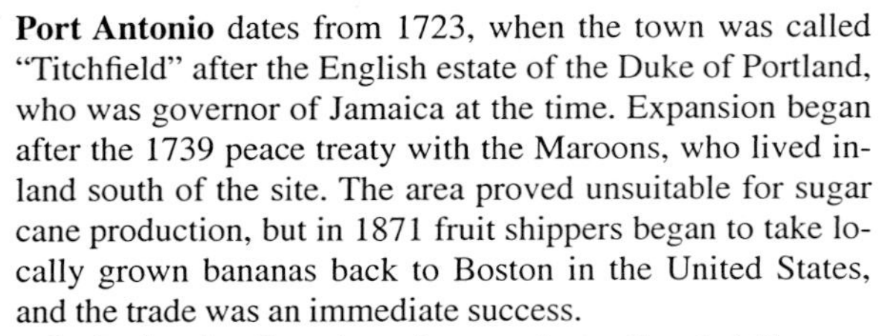

Port Antonio dates from 1723, when the town was called "Titchfield" after the English estate of the Duke of Portland, who was governor of Jamaica at the time. Expansion began after the 1739 peace treaty with the Maroons, who lived inland south of the site. The area proved unsuitable for sugar cane production, but in 1871 fruit shippers began to take locally grown bananas back to Boston in the United States, and the trade was an immediate success.

In its heyday Port Antonio was the undisputed "banana capital of the world," with an additional benefit: the banana boats brought the first tourists to Jamaica. The visitors traveled out on the empty boat and stayed in the area after the ships took their ripening cargo back to the US or England. Only the rich could afford to travel in this style, and Port Antonio developed into a center for high-class tourism. Fine hotels catered to the visitors' every need, and the town reveled in the money brought in from abroad.

Those days are long gone, as is the booming banana market:

Port Antonio is no longer the banana hub or high-class tourist center it used to be, but its beauty is undiminished.

exports from South America broke the Caribbean monopoly in the 1970s. However, Port Antonio harbor still has a buzz of activity, especially in the harvesting season, as all of Jamaica's banana exports leave from here. The manual counting of the "hands" and "bunches" of bananas (recounted in Harry Belafonte's "Banana Boat Song") was mechanized in the 1960s, but the work of loading the boats is still labor intensive. Developments at Port Antonio include a modern 32-slip marina, designed to blend in with the town's architecture and the West Harbour's charm. The complex has good facilities catering to vessels up to 350 ft. **Port Antonio Yacht Club** is the center for sport fishing, and plays host to the International Blue Marlin Tournament annually in October, when the harbor is filled with sport-fishing boats from around the Caribbean.

Nestled against the Blue Mountains, the town has a beautiful setting. Two wide bays offer natural harbors, and tiny **Navy Island** sits just offshore. This was the island bought by Errol Flynn when he settled in Port Antonio in 1946; he used it merely as a garden extension for the large yacht he moored there. His drinking parties were legendary, and he is fondly remembered by older folks in the town as a charming rogue. Take the small ferry from the harbor to Navy Island, where you can walk through the woodland or sunbathe on the small beaches. The once-private Flynn house is now a hotel and restaurant.

The headland between the two main bays is called "**The Hill**"; here you will find the oldest part of town. The houses of wealthy Port Antonio residents sat away from the bustle of the busy port in a grid of seven or eight streets. This area has fallen into decay, but there are still vestiges of its fine history to be seen. Ornate ironwork now rusts, wooden fretwork molds, and paint peels, yet there remains a beauty

A sweeping view of lush hills and brilliant coastline can be had from Port Antonio's Bonnie View Hotel.

about this aging finery. Nearby on St. George's Street is **St. George's Village**, an area of galleries and cafés designed as a quirky "Amsterdam street meets Italian piazza" mall. The whole idea is the brainchild of a German baroness who also owns the Palace Hotel, one of the smartest in town.

On the eastern peninsula tip is **Folly**, the remains of a large mansion surrounded by legend and mystery. Locals will tell you that it was built for a rich American who brought his new bride to Jamaica. As he carried her over the threshold, the house began to collapse and she fled, leaving him forever; his business subsequently failed and he became a broken man. There are few grains of truth in this story. The mansion, a fine Neo-Classical Italian villa, was actually built for Alfred Mitchell, an American who lived here with his family for a number of years. Unfortunately, the cement used for its construction contained sea sand, which caused the iron reinforcing rods to corrode. This eventually weakened the structure and it collapsed. The house now lies covered in undergrowth and makes a cattle pen for a local family, but remnants of the pretty arches and columns can still be seen.

For a wonderful view of the whole town, take the road up to **Bonnie View Hotel** (closed). The twin harbours, Navy Island, and the Hill can be seen from here. Don't forget your camera.

The **Rio Grande**, just west of Port Antonio, is the largest river complex on Jamaica, combining a number of tributaries from the Blue Mountains. Rafts have long been a method of transport for local people, who use them to carry bananas down from the upper slopes to the port. **Rafting** on the Rio Grande was popularized by Errol Flynn, who loved the adventure, and became a "must" for tourists in the late 1940s—it is still just as popular today. The lush river valley cuts deep into the heart of the mountains, with sheltered habitats for many birds and butterflies. A raft trip here is a much more tropical experience than on the Martha Brae River (farther west, at Falmouth). Rafters start at Berridale and complete their cruise at Rafters' Rest (St. Margaret's Bay), where there is a restaurant. There are even moonlight cruises for those who are romantically inclined.

Tropical Peace and Splendor

The drive east from Port Antonio offers some of the prettiest views in Jamaica. A series of coral headlands covered in tropical vegetation reach out into the ocean. Beautiful private villas and a small number of fine resort hotels sit proudly on the headlands or nestle in the small bays. **San San** gained a reputation in the days of Errol Flynn for its elegant social scene; today it is an exclusive hideaway with a fine golf course. A small faded sign points the way to **Blue Lagoon**, a tiny coastal inlet with a freshwater spring just offshore. The clear fresh water mixes with the briny sea water just a few meters away and creates a hundred hues of green and blue. The freshwater hole is said to be bottomless, although Jacques Cousteau dived here and measured the depth at 61 m (200 ft). You can swim and scuba-dive among a wealth of fish and other sea life; also, the bar and restaurant provide refreshment ranging from a drink to a three-course meal. **Frenchman's Cove**, a little farther east, is also beautiful. Tiny bays of soft sand sheltered by cliffs and cooling vegetation provide a completely different experience from the beaches of Montego Bay. This is the area for romantic private getaways.

To the south of the coastal area, **Athenry Gardens** (formerly a plantation) has wonderful views of the surrounding mountains, but these botanical gardens are renowned much more for what is under the ground than what is above it. The **Nonsuch Caves** have nine chambers with dramatic formations of stalactites and stalagmites. The largest cave is called the Cathedral because of its size and scale. You'll find fossils of fish and

Egrets line up before dinner on a small fishing boat in Boston Bay, Jamaica's traditional center of "jerk."

other marine creatures that were deposited in sediment millions of years ago, when this area lay on the ocean floor. The paths are well lit and offer amazing views of the interior.

Jamaica's Eastern Tip

If you continue along the main coastal road, you'll reach **Boston Bay**. This small fishing town at the easternmost end of the island is the traditional center of "jerk," Jamaica's national dish that is now gaining a worldwide following. The jerk marinating technique was first developed by the Maroon people as a method of tenderizing and cooking their pork. You will smell the roasting meat and aromatic wood fires as you arrive in the village. The fresh pork is cut into "bellies" and scored to make it easier to cook and serve. It is then covered in the paste that gives jerk its name, placed on a rack over the pit fire, and turned every few minutes until it is ready. The marinade is a good deal spicier than you would find in a tourist restaurant, but the meat is wonderfully tender; ask for a bite-sized sample before you buy. You'll be offered a serving of roasted breadfruit along with the jerk to provide the perfect bland antidote to the spice. Share the dining table in a simple shack with a few local families and you'll have one of those "real" Jamaican experiences.

The Maroon community, descendants of proud and tenacious slaves, still live in two isolated pockets on Jamaica. **Moore Town** and **Cornwall Barracks**, both inland from Boston Bay, make up the nucleus of the eastern group (the western Maroon area is in Cockpit Country, south of Falmouth). The settlements here were founded in 1739 after the peace treaty with the British. Maroon people are very private, still running their own affairs and paying no land taxes to the government. Although their villages don't look very different from the other rural communities on the island, it is the Maroon attitude to life which make these societies interesting to visit. If you wish to get to know the people, you can arrange to visit them with a guide (see page 119).

The coastal road makes its way around the eastern tip of Jamaica. The few attractions here are natural, very beautiful, and unspoiled, but the difficult and long journey from the major resorts means that few visitors venture this far. **Long Bay** is one of the longest and most magnificent beaches on the island, with not a hotel in sight—just nature at its best. There is no development here for two main reasons. First, this sector of coastline is most at risk from the threat of hurricanes as they whip across the Atlantic Ocean. Second, the coastal swells here are extremely dangerous, preventing the swimming activities and water sports so beloved by visitors. You'll find wooden fishing boats pulled up on the sands and nets hanging out to dry. The beach has fine pink sand; powerful breakers throw sea spray into the air. At the southern end of the beach is a small bar where you can sit and admire the dramatic view.

Farther south, near the fishing village of Manchioneal, are

Reach Falls (also known as Reich Falls), perhaps the last uncommercialized falls on Jamaica. The surrounding vegetation is truly tropical, with no landscaped lawns and no sign of a shopping village. The fresh clear water comes directly down from the mountains of the John Crow National Park and fall into a deep azure pool. Scenes in the film *Cocktail* (starring Tom Cruise) were filmed in the cascades.

On the easternmost tip of Jamaica stands **Morant Point Lighthouse**, built in 1841. With pristine mangrove swamps and the deserted sandy beaches of **Holland Bay** and **Mammee Bay**, the landscape is truly magnificent. The land stretches out for miles, but unfortunately, there is nobody here to hand you a cooling drink at the end of your exploration—and the difficult journey from the main road to the lighthouse makes it thirsty work indeed.

From Morant Point, the road turns west back toward Kingston. There is little to hold the attention here although the area has seen important historical events. **Port Morant**, a little way west, was the place where Captain Bligh of "The Bounty" fame first landed breadfruit on Jamaica. The famous mutiny occurred during the first journey, when he refused the crew much-needed water, keeping it instead for the precious plants. Even after all his effort, however, only one plant survived, and he had to return with a second cargo. It proved to be worth the effort for Bligh, who received a reward of 1,500 guineas for his effort.

Morant Bay is the major settlement in southeast Jamaica; it played a major part in one of the turning points in the history of the island. The Morant Bay rebellion of 1865 was led by Paul Bogle and supported by George William Gordon (after whom Gordon House, the Jamaican seat of Government, is named). The uprising and the violent reaction of the British forces resulted in the destruction of many of the historic

View of the Blue Mountains, famous for their tropical splendor and world-renowned coffee beans.

buildings in the town, which never really recovered. The most interesting attraction is a statue that commemorates Bogle, located outside the tiny courthouse. This strong, powerful depiction was designed and sculpted by Edna Manley.

The Blue Mountains

The **Blue Mountains** are the highest on Jamaica and cover much of the interior of the eastern part of the island. There are five major peaks: Blue Mountain Peak is the highest at 2,256 m (7,402 ft), and John Crow Mountain is the lowest at 1,753 m (5,750 ft). The mountains are blanketed with thick, verdant forests watered by regular tropical downpours from the heavy clouds that surround the high peaks. The blue heat haze that surrounds the mountains and gives them their name can best be seen on warm afternoons, when it is possible to see peak after peak stretching into the distance.

A number of slopes and valleys have remained untouched by man and offer a habitat for rare flora and fauna including the streamertail hummingbird, the national bird, and the giant swallowtail butterfly *(Papilio homerus)*, the second largest in the world. The richness of the environment around the Blue Mountains has long been recognized; protecting the areas of virgin forest is a priority. The **Blue and John Crow Mountains National Park**, was established in 1993 to manage and protect 78,200 hectares (193,200 acres) of land being damaged by illegal loggers and slash and burn farmers.

The best way to view the Blue Mountains is to drive from Buff Bay on the north coast down to Kingston on the B1 highway, although the road can be impassable after a heavy rain due to landslides. Always check with drivers and hotel employees to determine if road conditions are good before you depart. But the interior of the mountain range and the most beautiful parts of the parks are not accessible to vehicles: the best way to experience them is to take a guided walk. There are a variety of routes, which can last from a morning to several days. The hike to the summit of **Blue Mountain** itself is not for the inexperienced and will take a full day; if you want to see the sunrise, start out at 2am to reach the summit in time to greet another Jamaica day (see page 92). Whichever option you choose, remember to take some warm clothing, because temperatures here are a few degrees lower than on the coast, even on a sunny day. When the clouds come in, it can feel quite chilly. Visitors planning to overnight in the mountains should contact the Jamaica Conservation and Development Trust (see page 109).

In addition to their tropical splendor, the Blue Mountains have slopes at an altitude above 3,000 m (9,840 ft), which are perfect for growing coffee. In fact, Blue Mountain coffee is said by aficionados to be the best in the world. The **coffee plantations** lie in the humid heights, where soil conditions and the slow growing process (five years from germination to harvesting) produce a fine crop with a high yield. This natural affinity between the Blue Mountains and the coffee bean is amazing, because the first plants are said to have arrived in Jamaica by accident. In 1723 Louis XV of France ordered three *arabica* coffee plants to be sent from Yemen to the French island of Martinique, which lies farther south. Two plants died on the long journey and the third found its way to Jamaica—exactly how is still shrouded in mystery. This plant was the start of the Jamaican coffee industry, the most important business in this part of the island for more than 250 years. Because of the topography and the delicate nature of the plants, much of the work is still done by hand and traditional working practices have endured. The **Jablum Coffee Factory** near **Mavis Bank** offers guided tours where you can see beans being roasted and ground; you can also buy coffee beans to take home.

KINGSTON AND ENVIRONS

With one of the largest natural harbors in the world—lying between lush green hills and the Caribbean Sea—Kingston Bay became the perfect site for one of the biggest ports in the Caribbean. Commercial success made **Kingston** the capital of Jamaica in 1872.

Now home to more than 700,000 people (one-third of the population of Jamaica), it is a huge city with many facets. Modern "New Kingston," with its office buildings and high rise blocks, is the administrative heart of Jamaica, with government offices, consulates, and boutiques. To the northeast lie the foothills of the Blue Mountain range, where wealthy Kingstonians built houses to take advantage of the cooling breezes. The poor live on the flat, dusty plains below, where country life has simply been transplanted to the city. Goats wander the streets and people live in tiny tin shacks with few amenities. They sit up against several other shacks that make up blocks of properties (or "yards"). The violence and crime that have been a feature of life in Kingston over the years, center on political and gang rivalries within these yards.

Kingston's sites and attractions show the visitor how the island evolved both as a colony and as an independent country. They also provide insight into how Jamaicans view themselves and their culture with national pride.

Downtown

Downtown Kingston, once a model of British colonial "pomp and circumstance," is now surrounded by some of the poorest and most densely populated neighborhoods in the city. It is

Jamaica Highlights

Kingston and Vicinity *Appleton Distillery* (Siloah, St. Elizabeth, tel: 963-2210), open Monday–Saturday 9am–4pm. *Black River Safari* (by Black River Bridge, Black River, tel: 965-2573), daily cruises at 9am, 11am, 2pm, and 4pm. *Bob Marley Museum* (56 Hope Road, New Kingston, tel: 927-7056), open Monday–Saturday 9:30am–4pm. *Castleton Botanical Gardens* (on the A3 road), open daily 9am–6pm. *Devon House* (26 Hope Road, New Kingston, tel: 924-6603), open Tuesday–Saturday 10am–5pm, Sunday 11am–4pm. *Fort Charles* (Port Royal, tel: 923-9774), open Monday–Friday 9am–4pm, Saturday and Sunday 10am–5pm. *Jablum Coffee Factory* (Mavis Bank, tel: 997-8005), visits by appointment only. *Spanish Town Archaeological Museum* and *Jamaica Peoples Museum* (The Parade, Spanish Town), open Monday–Friday, 10am–4pm. *The National Gallery* (12 Ocean Boulevard, Kingston, tel: 922-1561), open Monday–Saturday 10am-5pm. *Taino Museum* open Monday–Thursday 9am–5pm, Friday 9am–4pm. *YS Falls* (Middle Quarters, St. Elizabeth, tel: 997-6055), open Tuesday–Sunday 9:30am–3:30pm, closed on public holidays.

A roadside orange seller in Kingston basks in the sun waiting for customers.

not a place to wander around without a guide. The risk of petty crime is high and the atmosphere is a little too oppressive for most tourists to feel comfortable walking the streets alone (see page 114).

The downtown area developed around the waterfront. Fruit, rum, and spices were once transported from the old docks; today the harbor area has been transformed. In 1982, the government built the **Jamaica Conference Centre**; there are also galleries and historical collections that celebrate the culture of the island. The **National Gallery**, on Ocean Boulevard, has a comprehensive collection of Jamaican paintings, sculpture, and other art, including works from the 1920s; there are many works by Edna Manley, one of the foremost modern artists on the island and wife of Norman Manley, former Prime Minister. Beside the docks is **Victoria Craft Market**, the domain of the famous "higglers," the assertive women who run the small stalls. The building, constructed in 1872, is a fine example of Victorian colonial architecture.

Away from the waterfront, the streets of the downtown area feature a number of historic buildings that are best visited as part of a guided tour (JUTA is the provider; see page 119). On Duke Street you will find **Headquarters House**, built in 1755.

The house became the property of the British military in 1814 and was selected as the seat of the island legislature in 1872, when the capital was moved from Spanish Town to Kingston. Nearby **Gordon House**, built in 1960, is the home to today's legislators; it was named after George William Gordon, leader of the Morant Bay rebellion, who became a member of the Jamaica Assembly and spoke out for the rights of the poor and oppressed. National Heroes Park, at the north end of Duke Street, used to be a racetrack (you can still make out the shape

Bargaining with Jamaica's "Higglers"

You'll meet these persuasive salespeople all over Jamaica, at craft markets or on the beaches. Their goal is to sell you the souvenir that you can't leave Jamaica without. However, since there are no set prices, you must engage in the intricate game of "haggling" if you want to buy and not get ripped off.

Many tourists feel uncomfortable having to negotiate a price, but it really is expected to be an enjoyable process. The main purpose is to agree on a fair price for both the purchaser and the vendor. If you have your heart set on a particular article, then it will be possible to find an amicable agreement. Prices will vary with the season: low season means greater flexibility on price.

Don't get into a haggling situation if you are really not interested in buying an article. It only creates bad feelings, and you may feel the sharp edge of a "patois" tongue. These people are trying to earn a living and don't want to waste time. They would rather have a firm but honest "No" than five minutes of negotiation followed by no sale. They view this as disrespect for them on your part.

As a guideline, aim to start your negotiation at about half the initial price offered. Sale price should generally be about 20 percent lower than the vendor's original offer.

Devon House, original home of Jamaica's first black millionaire, George Steibel.

of the circuit). Monuments to the heroes of independent Jamaica can be found in a small corner of the park, and both Marcus Garvey and Norman Manley are buried here.

The Institute of Jamaica, on East Street, was founded in 1879 to encourage research in science, art, and literature in the true spirit of the Victorian age. It has the largest collection of books, articles, and papers on the history of the West Indies in the world and is an important archive for students and academics. Many branch sections of the institute are located across the city, including the **Natural History Museum** (on Tower Street), the oldest museum on the island, with a collection of over 125,000 types of preserved plant species.

King Street is the heart of the downtown area and the main shopping street. Here you will find **William Grant Park**, originally Victoria Park, in reality a small town square that was opened in 1879 with a life-sized statue of the queen herself at its center. In 1977 it was renamed after the black nationalist leader. The **Parade**, the streets surrounding the park, once heard the marching steps of British soldiers; it was here that slaves were beaten or hanged as punishment for their "crimes." Now it is a hive of "higgler" activity and lives by the beat of reggae music. It is also the hub for bus routes around the city.

New Kingston

New Kingston is the modern commercial center of the Corporate Area (parishes of Kingston and St. Andrew), and is the hub of business, with hotels, fast food places and night spots. Near the Jamaica Pegasus hotel is **Emancipation Park**, popular with the lunch crowd in the day and joggers in the evening.

On the edge of the district is **Devon House**, built in 1881 as a plantation house for George Steibel, the first black millionaire of Jamaica. Restored in 1967, the beautiful exterior is complemented by the fine period furniture housed inside. The gardens make a cooling place to sit after a guided tour, and the equally alluring cafés and a renowned restaurant offer a range of refreshments. Nearby on Hope Road are **Jamaica House**, containing the offices of the Prime Minister; **Vale Royal**, the Prime Minister's official residence; and **King's House**, home

A Kingston wall painting of the great Bob Marley is one of many memorials that are scattered throughout Jamaica.

of the Governor General, originally the residence of the Bishop of Jamaica. None of these buildings are open to the public.

Tuff Gong Recording Studios used to be located at 56 Hope Road, a small compound where reggae musician, Bob Marley, lived and worked. Since his death it has been transformed into the **Bob Marley Museum** and managed by the Marley family to protect the memory of his life. The museum has some interesting displays, including Marley's gold records and photographs of activity at the studios. Some of his personal effects can be found in the modest bedroom where he slept. The museum is open daily (except Sunday); guided tours only.

Port Royal

A spit of land reaches out south of the city across Kingston Bay, sheltering the famous harbor. Called the **Palisadoes** (after the Spanish word *palisade*, meaning "defense"), this is an arid area of magnificent cacti and margins of mangrove that shelter populations of seabirds. Halfway along the narrow peninsula you'll find **Sangster International Airport**, the main airport of entry for Kingston and the eastern part of the island. At the tip of the Palisadoes is Port Royal.

The Spanish never settled this strip of land, but when the British arrived in the late 1650s they built Fort Cromwell here; it was renamed **Fort Charles** following the restoration of the British monarchy in 1662. Within a few years **Port Royal**, the town surrounding the fort, earned a reputation as the most raucous and debauched city in the Caribbean. With the help of the pirates who made the town their base, Port Royal became a very rich city, with the income from sugar and rum combined with stolen Spanish treasure (see page 18). After the 1692 earthquake that devastated the city and buried much of its wealth, Port Royal never fully recovered. Only some of its treasures have been salvaged (along with everyday articles

Sport-fishing boats dock at the marina of Port Royal, a town rich in maritime history.

such as pewter cutlery and plates); much still lies only a few feet below the waves. You can explore for yourself by diving at the site; contact Morgan's Harbour Hotel for more details.

Kingston replaced Port Royal as the commercial center of the island. However, Fort Charles was rebuilt as a military and naval garrison, and it protected Jamaica and much of the English Caribbean for 250 years until the advent of steamships and yet another earthquake in 1907 saw its decline. The brick fort, home to Lord Horatio Nelson during 1779, still stands proud and "ship-shape." The large cannons on the battlements now guard **Fort Charles Maritime Museum**, which documents the maritime history of Jamaica. Here you can view models both of the fort and of the types of ships that sailed the Caribbean over the centuries.

Landslides and small quakes have taken their toll on sites at the Fort, and **Giddy House** is a perfect example of this. The small, square building once stored ordnance, but after years of seismic activity—particularly the destructive 1907 earthquake—it has been left at a very precarious angle, sinking back into the sand. The sadly dilapidated **Old Naval Hospital** can be found a little farther to the north; its distinctive iron supports were brought to Jamaica in 1819 and were designed to be both earthquake and hurricane proof. The hospital building now houses the **National Archaeological and Historical Museum**, which displays a fascinating collection of finds from the sunken city of Port Royal but, sadly, very little pirate treasure. Equally interesting are the displays that examine the methods of marine archaeology used to excavate the city.

Residents of the little village of Port Royal now make their living from fishing. On weekends, it's a popular place for families from Kingston to come to enjoy the fresh air or a fantastic fried fish dinner at one of the little restaurants that spill out into the streets. Scenes from the James Bond film *Doctor No* were filmed at the **Morgan's Harbour Hotel**, which also

Jamaica's Predator Pest

If you travel around the island at all, you are bound to catch sight of a mongoose running across the road into the undergrowth. This small furry creature was introduced to Jamaica during colonial times to prey on snakes and rats, which were a danger both to the people and to the crops. The mongoose was extremely successful in ridding the island of these two problems. However, it then began to look for other things to eat. It is now considered to be the most populous and vicious pest on the island, preying on domestic chickens as well as eating the eggs and chicks of native wild birds.

celebrates the life of its namesake, pirate-turned-Lieutenant Governor Henry Morgan. In the small marina you can eat while surrounded by expensive boats. From here you can also take an inexpensive short trip to **Lime Cay**, which lies just to the south of the tip of Port Royal. This tiny "desert island" offers the opportunity to sunbathe on sandy shores or snorkel in clear water and feel a million miles away from Kingston.

CENTRAL HIGHLANDS AND THE SOUTH COAST

Away from the large towns and tourist resorts, life continues in time-honored tradition. In central and south Jamaica, numerous small settlements and family farms dot the countryside, where you'll see donkeys tethered at the roadside or trotting along the lanes carrying large baskets. A network of smaller roads that knit the villages together make traveling a real adventure: there are few signposts (and even fewer people) to point the way if you do become lost.

The contrast between the landscape of the central highlands and the south coast could not be more marked. The highlands are cool, with verdant hills rolling through the heart of Jamaica. As you travel south, the landscape changes. Acres of grassland surround coral limestone columns and escarpments. Low-growing acacia trees replace tropical vegetation, with the landscape characterized much more by prairie than by palm trees. The southern-most margins of the island—away from the pressure of human development—are a haven for wildlife.

Spanish Town

The Spanish settlers in 16th-century Jamaica, having tired of the disease-ridden Nueva Sevilla in the north, looked for a new site for their capital city. They chose the flatlands around the Rio Cobre and, in 1534, established Villa de la Vega, whose name was later changed to St. Jago de la Vega. Unfortunately for the Spanish, the British captured Jamaica in 1655 and henceforth gave the settlement the rather unimaginative name "Spanish Town." As capital of a wealthy colony, Spanish Town had its fair share of fine buildings that included courthouses, administrative offices, and official residences. However, the capital was moved in 1872 to Kingston, the commercial heart of Jamaica, and a malaise enveloped Spanish Town from which it never recovered.

There are plans to restore the elegant Georgian buildings along the **Parade**, which have fallen into disrepair, and to upgrade the town center. The most striking building in the Parade is the white stone edifice that houses the **Rodney Memorial**, constructed in gratitude after Admiral Rodney's fleet saved Jamaica by defeating the French at the Battle of Les Saintes in 1782. The building cost much more than the budget allocated for it at the time but is, as a result, a truly spectacular monument. One wing houses the **Jamaica Archives and Records Office**, which preserves original documents from throughout the island's history.

On the west side of the square is **Old King's House** (built in 1762), which was the official residence of the British governor; it was here that the proclamation of emancipation was issued in 1838. It was a fine building but has never been recovered from a disastrous fire in 1925. **The Jamaican People's Museum of Craft and Technology**, housed in a reconstructed corner of the house, features a model of how the building looked before the fire.

Two miles east of Spanish Town, the **Taino Museum** comprises the most important collection of Arawak artifacts in Jamaica. The museum re-creates the Arawak lifestyle in a series of models illustrating how villages and daily activities might have looked. It is sad to think that this peaceful culture

The Rodney Memorial buildings recall the town's official capacity, before the capital moved to Kingston.

survived in Jamaica for 800 years, only to disappear within 30 years of the arrival of European colonists.

The **Hellshire Hills**, south of Spanish Town, come as a surprise to those who think that the tropics can only be lush and green. The landscape here is underscored by limestone and receives fewer than 760 mm (30 inches) of rain per year. There is little soil to support plants, resulting in a desert-like landscape of cactus and low scrub trees. The area has become the last haven for many of the native but almost extinct plants, animals, and birds of Jamaica. Here you'll find the last few Jamaican iguanas and yellow snakes. The string of beaches along the coast are popular destinations for Kingstonians on weekends.

Mandeville

Mandeville sits to the west of Spanish Town in the Don Figuero Mountains. Its cool air and pretty setting made it a favorite retreat for colonial families right up to the end of British rule in

Visitors relax in one of the pools at YS Falls, a stunning site for aquatic fun and recreation.

Jamaica in 1962. They came to spend their weekends here, away from the hot and humid atmosphere of Kingston. Today it is a favorite place for wealthy Jamaican families for very much the same reason. The town was laid out in 1816 and named for Lord Mandeville, the eldest son of the Duke of Manchester, after whom Manchester Parish was named. The English modeled the town and its buildings on those of their homeland, and one can imagine the village greens, tennis and golf clubs, and grassy verges taken from a typical London suburb.

There are a number of interesting attractions lying to the west of Mandeville. One of the most popular—and thus on the itinerary of many tours—is **Appleton Distillery**, situated in rolling hills just to the south of Cockpit Country. Sugar cane was brought to Jamaica by the Spanish in the early 16th century, and much of the crop was exported. But it was treated before being shipped, and a by-product of the treatment was molasses, used as a basis for making rum. Many major sugar factories had a distillery on site, usually producing alcohol for local consumption. Appleton Distillery went one step further and produced, arguably, the best rum in the world. The plant, which has been in operation since 1749, produces 42,000 liters (74,000 pints) of rum every day in 150-year-old stills. Much of this is "overproof" rum, the basis of intoxicating rum punches. But the finest rum is aged in casks for up to 30 years to produce a spirit comparable to brandy or cognac. The distillery offers a tour of the rum plant and the opportunity to taste and buy a range of rum and rum-based drinks. It can also provide lunch in the restaurant if you phone in advance.

In some parts of the island, bamboo was planted along the roadside to provide shelter for people traveling in the heat of the day. The groves of bamboo also created places where slaves would congregate without being seen by their colonial masters. Much of the bamboo was allowed to decay or was torn up later in Jamaica's history, but **Bamboo Avenue**, the one remaining section, can be found on the main A2 road between Mandeville and Black River. It is a 3-km (2-mile) tunnel of bamboo surrounded by sugar cane, with somnolent grazing cattle tethered along its length.

Nearby are **YS Falls**, found on an old plantation that dates from 1684. The water cascades 50 m (164 ft) over three major falls and has formed two large pools as well as a small cave system at the base of the second drop. It is not possible to walk up through the water as at Dunn's River, but steps have been erected at the side of the water to take you to a platform at the foot of the first cascade. You can swim in the pools at each level, and a rope swing has been created at the middle level for those who want to try their hand at being Tarzan. The falls are surrounded by native forests and tropical flowers, but an area of grassy lawn has been created for sunbathing and picnicking. There are changing rooms and a small refreshment area. It is said that the falls got their name from the initials of the two original landowners, John Yates and Colonel Richard Scott. The cattle and sugar barrels exported from the plantation in fact had these initials branded onto them. Others say that the original name for the falls was the "Wyaess," which is said to mean "winding." Whichever is true, the YS Falls make a beautiful attraction for an hour or a whole day of fun.

Black River

Once a major port on the south coast, **Black River** is now a small, sleepy town on the banks of the river from which it took its name. Its industry was the export of red logwood and the dyes of indigo and Prussian blue, which were extremely valuable in Britain. There is still some fine Georgian architecture here, but most visitors come to see the **Great Morass Mangrove Swamp**. This area, which should not be confused with the Great Morass near Negril, is about 6,500 hectares (16,000 acres) of freshwater and tidal wetlands. The Mangrove Swamp and rush beds are an important habitat for many species of birds

A pontoon boat motors through Black River's Great Morass Mangrove Swamp.

and fish, as well as home to a small population of Jamaican crocodiles. Smaller than the Florida species and said to be more docile, they grow to 6 m (20 ft) in length and can live to an age of 100 years.

The Black River, at 71 km (44 miles), is the longest in Jamaica; it was an arterial route used to transport rum and lumber from the inland plantations. It still provides a living for many families, either from fishing or from the harvesting of bull-rushes for basket making. Tours on the river and into the Great Morass start from Black River town (see page 90). The route takes you into the **Mangrove Alley**, said to be the quietest place in Jamaica, where you can search out the basking reptiles and native birds that call this place home. Roots, which look like cathedral organ pipes, drop from the higher trees. Your guide will turn off the engine and an eerie silence will envelop the boat. The highlight of the trip is the visit to see "Charlie," a 4-m (13-ft) crocodile who swims up to the boat when called. The guide assured us that he had gone swimming in the water near Charlie without fear of being attacked, but testing this statement is not recommended.

Treasure Beach

The southern coastline of Jamaica has so far resisted the pressure from big developers, partly because it has few main roads. Environmentalists work hard to protect the unspoiled beauty and wildlife habitats. Those who do venture here are rewarded with beautiful scenery and friendly people. **Treasure Beach** is the only resort area to speak of, with just a handful of hotels stretching across three sandy bays. One such place is the funky and stylishly-designed Jake's. The local population of St. Elizabeth Parish still makes a living from fishing, and their wooden boats rest high on the dark, volcanic sand. You'll be able to spend the day relaxing

Charlie's an angel—Black River's most famous resident greets passengers on passing pontoon boats.

without being hassled. If you want to buy a souvenir, just hail the mobile shop that drives slowly along the road looking for customers. There's very little to do here but chill out.

East of Treasure Beach are some beautifully natural strips of coastline. On one strip is the Little Ochi seafood restaurant, a simple affair in the fishing village of **Alligator Pond**. Popular with locals and visitors alike, people travel from as far away as Ocho Rios, just to sample the cuisine. The government-owned **Alligator Hole** (also known as Canoe Valley Wetland) on the eastern side of Long Bay has been awarded official status for protection of the last remaining manatee population on Jamaica. This pristine region of freshwater and saltwater swamps, edged with limestone cliffs, offers a refuge to this gentle creature as well as to birds and land crabs.

NEGRIL AND THE WEST

This area, the farthest from Kingston, lagged behind other parts of Jamaica in modern development, protected from the commercial activity of the east by the limestone landscape of Cockpit Country, making travel and communication difficult. It was an outpost of pirate activity in the 17th and 18th centuries. Today, Negril is at the forefront of the tourist industry.

Heading west from Montego Bay, the main road hugs the coastline. Just a little way out of town is **Tryall Estate**. This old pineapple plantation had fallen into decline before being transformed into the first (and some say the best) resort hotel on the island. Although the clubhouse and historic great house are camouflaged by lush vegetation, the manicured greens of the golf course can be seen on both sides of the main coast road, along with the plantation's water wheel, which has been renovated and still turns with the weight of river water. A number of golf tournaments are held here every year.

Negril

A pirate hideaway in the 1600s, **Negril** was rediscovered in the 1960s by the "children of love" and others looking for an alternative lifestyle. It is now one of *the* places in the world for relaxed, bohemian vacations. Jamaicans say that Negril isn't a place—it's "a state of

A signpost tells visitors to Negril exactly where they stand in this world.

mind" where almost anything goes. There are few hippies left today, but the pleasures are still pretty earthy: it's not unusual to see topless sunbathers or catch a faint whiff of "aromatic" smoke. You're also much more likely to see true Rastafarians here, along with many others who simply enjoy living the image of the religion without abiding by its strict rules. Dreadlocks and tams (colorful knitted hats) are everywhere, along with the passing salutations. Located on the western tip of Jamaica, Negril is also one of the best places in the world for watching the sun go down before heading out for a night on the town.

The spot is interesting also because of its topographical personality. To the east is Long Bay, a vast expanse of fantastic sandy beach, while to the west is West End, with coral cliffs that drop directly into the clear blue ocean. Town planning regulations limit the height of buildings to tree-top level, creating an open and natural look and feel throughout the town. Resort hotels and innumerable bars and restaurants are camouflaged and shaded by the cooling vegetation.

☛ **Long Bay** is seven miles of sublime fine sand, gentle azure water, and cooling palm trees. It is one of the best beaches in the Caribbean, and many large resort hotels have

Negril's West End, where coral cliffs drop directly into the clear blue ocean, is perfect for snorkeling.

been built here to take advantage of it. You may find that you don't want to leave your hotel when you can spend the day being waited on hand and foot, but Long Bay also has a number of lively bars and restaurants to enjoy. There are also water sports galore if you have the energy.

Because parts of Long Bay beach are public, you'll meet many local people here, probably more than in any other

View from Rick's Café, Negril's favorite vantage point for enjoying the sunset with a cold drink.

resort area in Jamaica. Vendors and hair braiders are sure to approach you. Although official braiders can be found in pink booths along the beach, any number of "unofficial" ladies can be found at the cafés and bars. The soothing aloe that they apply while you sunbathe will be sure to cost you a small tip. There are endless rows of small craft stalls under the palm trees, but the craft market at the town end of Long Bay has everything in one place. You'll be able to buy a sarong for the beach or choose a wooden carving to take home with you.

At the top of Long Bay is **Booby Cay**, a small island just a short distance offshore. The tree-topped rock surrounded by golden sandy beaches is the archetypal "desert island"—a great place for snorkeling, sunbathing, or picnics. You can rent a canoe to get there under your own steam or take a ride in one of the many small ferry boats departing from Long Bay.

The coral cliffs of **West End** provide a total contrast to Long Bay. Diving and snorkeling are the things to do here, and the shimmering waters house some wonderful sea life. If you have never tried diving before, many companies offer training to recognized professional standards. West End is also the place to take in the **sunset**. Almost everyone heads to **Rick's Café**, perched on the cliff top, to have a drink and set up the camera. While you're waiting, you'll be entertained by the divers who launch themselves from the tops of tiny perches into the azure sea some 9 m (30 ft) below. They are often joined by courageous tourists, who usually get more applause than do the professionals. If you're without a car, taking a sunset cruise on a catamaran will transport you effortlessly to West End, and you can lie offshore away from the crowds with your rum punch. The cliff road ends at the Victorian-era **Old Lighthouse**, which still protects ships passing this rocky promontory.

To the east of Negril is the **Great Morass**, a wetland area covering around 2,400 hectares (5,900 acres). The wetland and the **Royal Palm Reserve** are managed by the Negril Area

Aloe Vera

As you lie on the beach, you are sure to be offered an aloe vera massage by a passing "higgler." You will be told that it will help you develop a golden tan, but be aware that aloe—although an excellent treatment for sunburn—should not be used as a tanning or sun-protection product. Make sure that you use a product with a suitably high SPF (Sunscreen Protection Factor) to protect your skin while you sunbathe.

Environmental Protection Trust (NEPT), which preserves one of the largest swathes of Royal Palm—Jamaica's national plant—left on the island. Numbers have dwindled due to the rapid development of past decades, but the 87 hectares (215 acres) of palms here are protected from exploitation and damage. The wetlands also support a large number of birds and land crabs. There have been attempts to drain the wetlands, but this damaged not only the Great Morass but also areas of the coral reef offshore. Both are now officially protected.

To the South

The road along the coastline to the south travels through busy agricultural towns and fishing villages untouched by tourism. The first settlement is **Little London**, which has a relatively large Indian population. The itinerant workers settled here to work their own farmland and now provide the markets with much of Jamaica's fresh produce. Next is **Savanna-la-Mar**, the bustling capital of Westmoreland Parish. The highlight here is **Mannings School** (built in 1738), which still retains its original colonial-style wooden buildings. These are beautifully preserved and painted in bright tropical colors, a perfect environment for the children in their smart uniforms. Nearby at Ferris Cross is **Paradise Park**, a working cattle ranch where many scenes from the film *Papillon* (starring Steve McQueen and Dustin Hoffman) were shot.

South of Savanna-la-Mar the road hugs the coast, here narrow beaches brim with faded wooden *pirogue* canoes and other boats. This is one of Jamaica's prime fishing areas, and around **Bluefields** you'll see local men carrying their catch home. The specialty of this region is spicy shrimp, caught and cooked within minutes at stalls along the roadside. Local women offer bags of this snack for a few dollars, but try one first before you buy—they can be very hot and spicy.

WHAT TO DO

Jamaica cannot claim to have the very best beaches, reefs, or sport fishing in the Caribbean. However, it is indeed one of the best "all-around" islands in the region, offering a wide range of opportunities for a variety of activities. Under the warm island sun you can enjoy water sports or you can just relax on the sand doing nothing at all. Nightlife includes an abundance of reggae music and dancing, and if you're here at the right time of year you can attend some of the world's biggest pop music festivals. For those in shopping mode, the choices are many: woodcarvings, colorful clothing, coffee, and (of course) rum. If your family or group includes those with different interests—or if you simply want something new to do every day—Jamaica is the perfect destination.

OUTDOOR RECREATION AND SPORTS

Beaches and Water Sports

Spending the day on the beach taking in the sun is one of the primary reasons tourists visit Jamaica. Every resort area has its own famous beaches with their own particular beauty. Negril has the great expanse of Long Bay and the small "desert

Parasailing is one of many exciting activities to offset heavy relaxation in Negril.

Take time out on the beach in Negril to get your hair braided by local experts.

island" of Booby Cay, while Montego Bay has the shorter expanses of Doctor's Cave Beach and Cornwall Beach. In Ocho Rios you will find Turtle Beach, where you can watch the cruise boats docking at the pontoon in the bay. Port Antonio beaches are now the domains of the fine hotels on San San Bay, Frenchman's Cove, and Dragon Bay, all of which are tiny coves protected by rocky tropical outcrops. Long Bay on the eastern coast is wonderful because it is remote and uncrowded, but it is not suitable for swimming because of strong currents. Treasure Beach on the south coast has dark volcanic sand beaches that are home to colorful fishing boats.

At the major resorts, beaches are kept very clean and facilities for a range of water sports are readily available. Jet skiing is popular in the sheltered waters near the beaches. If you are adventurous, you can go parasailing, with a boat pulling you along above the beach and waterfront. This is particularly exciting along Long Bay at Negril—a perfect way to see the whole length of the beach without having to walk. A couple of resort bars have even installed large trampolines offshore, where you can swim out and spend some time bouncing above the water.

If you do intend to take part in any sporting activity, be sure to check that your travel insurance policy specifically covers it. Some policies have clauses that do not cover certain sports.

Snorkeling

Jamaica is particularly good for snorkeling, with many reefs and rocky promontories to explore very close to the shore. There are also a number of shallow areas between reefs that offer a fascinating view of various types of sea life. Beautiful tropical fish in iridescent blue and green search through the coral for food, and you'll be able to catch sight of the odd ray. All the major resorts have small boats offering trips to offshore sites if you want to snorkel in deeper water.

The West End at Negril is ideal for snorkeling. The coral cliffs drop down into a clear azure sea, and there are hundreds of caves and canyons to explore. Long Bay offers shallow snorkeling along the sandy bottom. Montego Bay has the Marine Park with a range of freshwater and seawater environments. Farther east, Runaway Bay comes into its own when you get into the water, offering a range of fine reefs running parallel to the line of hotels along the beach. Ocho Rios has a wonderful shallow reef running east from Turtle Beach for safe snorkeling.

The Jamaica Look

Hair-braiding, a very popular activity on the beaches, is a great way to show everyone you had a great Jamaican holiday. Braiding is a traditional technique first used in Africa to style hair, but today it is also fashionable for visitors while on the island. It is a cool style in a warm climate, and it's easy to care for during your stay. Just make sure that you protect the scalp between the braids for a few days to avoid sunburn.

Diving

Much of the northern coast of Jamaica is surrounded by areas of deep reef wall that make diving a pleasure. Although some sections of reef have been damaged in recent years, there are still many areas with a wide range of fish and other creatures to see. Most of the major resort areas offer diving opportunities and certified training facilities for those who want to learn how to dive. Your hotel may offer certified instruction or guided dives. If not, you can contact the Jamaica Tourist Board for a selection of approved and certified dive operators. Here is a short list of the best places for diving off the Jamaica coast:

Negril. Pete Wreck is an old submerged tug boat. Throne Room is a crack in the reef.

Montego Bay. Marine Park is surrounded by underwater walls of coral. Airport Reef and Widowmaker's Reef are areas of the wall.

Runaway Bay. In Ricky's Reef and Pockets Reef there are a couple of light aircraft that crashed and are now being colonized by sea creatures.

Ocho Rios. The reef wall drops over 900 m (nearly 3,000 ft) but comes close to shore, offering nearby dives with a wide variety of fish and other aquatic life.

Kingston. Lime Cay is a tiny island off Port Royal.

Boat Charters, River Tours, and Rafting

If you don't want to get into the water but you still want to see aquatic life on the reef, then take a glass-bottomed boat trip. There are a number of companies in all the major resorts. At Negril and Ocho Rios, the boats tie up along the main beach; you can negotiate a price while you sunbathe. The boats in Montego Bay all dock at the same place, so you can compare prices and facilities. Pier 1 has a range of options,

Calendar of Events

Exact dates vary. If you want to attend a particular event, be sure to check with the Jamaica Tourist Board before you book.

January *Accompong Maroon Festival* (Cockpit Country), held on 6 January. *High Mountain Coffee* 10K and 5K Road Race (Williamsfield). *Air Jamaica Jazz & Blues Festival* (Montego Bay).

February *Pineapple Cup Yacht Race,* from Miami to Montego Bay. *Bob Marley Birthday Bash,* held on 6 February (location varies).

March *West End Reggae Festival* (Negril). *Fun in the Son – Gospel Festival* (Ocho Rios).

April *Jamaica Carnival* (Kingston), the most lively and outrageous parade of the year. *Montego Bay Yacht Club Easter Regatta.*

May *Jake's Annual Jamaican Off-Road Triathlon* (Treasure Beach). *Calabash International Literary Festival* (Treasure Beach). A free event.

June *Ocho Rios Jazz Festival,* featuring top musicians.

August *Independence Day Parade* (Kingston/island wide), with street parades featuring *junkanoo* dancers. *Hi-Pro Family Polo Tournament and Horse Show* (Chukka Cove). *Reggae Sumfest* (Montego Bay).

September *Montego Bay Yacht Club Marlin Tournament. Negril Sprint Triathlon* (Long Bay Beach Park).

October *Port Antonio Blue Marlin Tournament,* a four-day tournament attracting sports fishermen from around the world. *Oktoberfest* (St. Andrew).

November *Jamaican Film and Music Festival* (Montego Bay).

December *Junkanoo* street celebrations in towns throughout the island, celebrating the approaching new year with paraders in costume.

Sand beyond the beach—golf courses can be found at the major resort hotels throughout Jamaica.

from small boats to large submersible craft that will take you under the water in complete comfort; try MoBay Undersea Tours (tel: 979-2281). If you are not a confident swimmer, a boat is the best way to enter this very different world.

For a relaxing ride down the Martha Brae River on a raft, tel: 952-0889. Take a trip down the Black River to experience the "Great Morass" and see crocodiles in action (contact Black River Safari, tel: 965-2513). Or you can simply get wet and picnic at YS Falls, near Mandeville (tel:. 997-6055).

Sport Fishing

Sport fishing is also a major activity. Port Antonio holds a major international tournament each October. Blue-and-white marlin are the prized catch, and the waters around Jamaica are especially rich in these magnificent fish. Other fish are plentiful: you only have to see what the local fishermen are bringing in. You will find sport fishing boats for hire at the marinas in the major resorts: Bay Pointe at Montego Bay, the main beach in Ocho Rios, Morgan's Harbour Hotel at Port Royal in Kingston, and the harbor at Port Antonio. You can hire a boat with equipment and crew by the day or half day.

Recreation on Land

Golf

Jamaica offers an excellent range of golf courses, from the hot, dry course at Negril to the breezy course at Mandeville in the center of the island. Several important tournaments take place during the year, where you can watch international players from the PGA and the LPGA compete.

Montego Bay is particularly well blessed with fine courses at the large resort hotels. These have been professionally designed and are maintained in peak condition. The most famous course is at the Tryall resort just west of Montego, where the greens caress the undulating coastal slopes. To the east of Montego Bay, where the coastal plain is flat and wide and an ideal landscape for golf, there are several large resort hotels that boast courses. Half Moon Golf Club, Wyndham Rose Hall Country Club, and Ironshore Golf and Country Club have all been created by internationally acclaimed designers and offer a challenge for all ability levels. These courses are open to the public.

Horseback Riding

There are several places in Jamaica to get in the saddle. Try the facilities at the Half Moon Hotel (tel: 953-2286) or the stables on the Barnett Estate (tel: 952-2382).

Walking and Hiking

Jamaica is a perfect island for walking or hiking, with a range of different environments from coastline to tropical peaks, from dry limestone landscapes to lush river valleys.

More and more visitors want to get off the beaten path, at least for part of their holiday.

A guide is recommended for a trek to the Blue Mountain Peak or a hike into the Cockpit Country. Several companies organise tours that can be tailored to your needs. The Southern Trelawny Environmental Association (STEA) provide local guides for Cockpit Country tours (tel: 610-0818). Valley Hikes (tel: 993-3881) and Grand Valley Tours (tel: 993-4116), based in Port Antonio, have a variety of hikes in the Rio Grande Valley and northern sections of the Blue and John Crow mountains. Sun Venture Tours run island-wide hiking, caving, safari and adventure tours (tel: 960-6685).

Spectator Sports

Spectator sports tend to be seasonal. Depending on the time of year, you can attend the following competitive events.

Cricket

This game is traditionally a mystery to all except the British and former British colonies. However, there are few things more genteel on a hot afternoon than watching a match unfold and hearing the sound of leather striking willow. Just make sure that you sit next to someone who can explain the rules. The professional season in Jamaica runs from January until August each year, but you might come across a local game in almost any village at any time. The English introduced cricket to the island, but Jamaican players and spectators bow to nobody in their obvious enthusiasm for the game.

Polo

Matches are played at Chukka Cove (tel: 972-2506) near St. Ann's Bay on the northern coast. The major tournaments take place in March and August.

Deep-Sea Sport Fishing

This is not an easy sport to watch, since the action happens at sea. But if you wait for the boats to come back to port at the end of the day, you can experience the excitement of the weigh-in and the photograph of the sportsman and his massive catch. Port Antonio has a major competition in October.

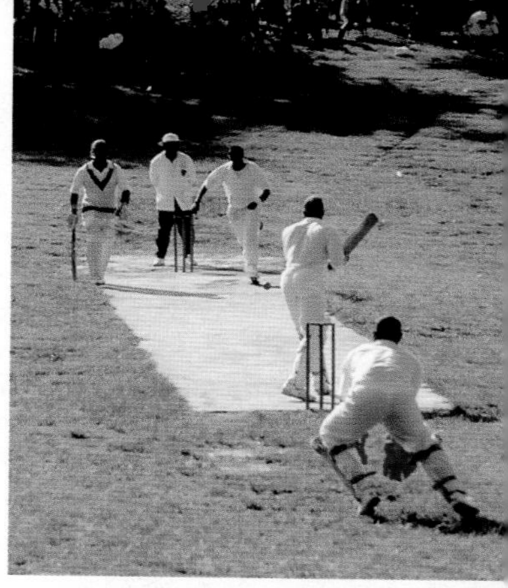

Cricket—being played by Mandeville locals—is part of Jamaica's British legacy.

Horse Racing

There is a track at Caymanas Park near Kingston. Betting is in Jamaican dollars only.

NIGHTLIFE AND ENTERTAINMENT

Jamaicans love the sound of live bands and really come alive when they listen (and dance) to the local music, of which there is a vast range. Reggae, with its strong and bouncy "backbeat," has been a huge influence on pop music throughout the world. Today Jamaica still has one of the most intense grassroots music traditions in the world, and its recording industry is competitive and quite lucrative.

You'll find live music in bars and restaurants every night of the week. These will usually be advertised in the free tourist magazines in your hotel's lobby, or out on the street on booming speaker systems placed on top of a car. If you want to go out into the night, Negril, Ocho Rios, and Montego Bay all have nightclubs that stay open very late.

The sweet sounds of Jamaica —a local musician plays guitar in Ocho Rios.

For something more formal, many hotels have Caribbean or Jamaican "nights" where you can watch a dance show and later do a little dancing yourself. These traditional evenings often feature the rhythms of the wider Caribbean, with music such as calypso (Trinidad) and *mérengue* (Dominican Republic).

There are many events that fill the night with the beat of Jamaican music. The island's biggest music festival is the "Reggae Sumfest", which is held at a variety of venues in Montego Bay each July/ August and features international and local artists; <www.montego-bay-jamaica.com/sumfest>. Ocho Rios also holds an annual international jazz festival. Check the Jamaica Tourist Board website <www.jamaicatravel.com> for details of these and other annual arts events; the What's On Jamaica website also has a weekly entertainment guide: <www.whatsonjamaica.com> .

SHOPPING

One thing that you notice about Jamaica is that many shops come to you. You won't be able to walk down the street without someone approaching you with crafts and other commodities. Buying from the street traders means there is no set price, and some people feel uncomfortable about haggling. Follow the advice on page 65 to increase your confidence and remember two things: bargaining is supposed to be an enjoyable interaction, and nobody can make you buy something that you don't want.

Art and crafts. The Jamaican people are highly skilled in the art of carving wood. It is one aspect of communal pride that has carried on since colonial times. Woodcarvings are a major souvenir product, and there is a huge range from fine carved pieces to objects in the rough "naive" style. Rastafarian faces and figures are a popular choice, as are such African animals as giraffe and elephants. You will see natural wood and also a range of colorful productions in the red, yellow, and green Rasta colors. It really is a matter of looking around and finding something you like. The wide range of styles is matched by an equally wide range of quality, so do check the pieces carefully before you buy. Different types of wood have different weights and different finishes. Some of the pieces are extremely lightweight, but the dark *lignum vitae* wood is heavy and has a beautiful finish when carved. Don't buy articles if the wood still looks green: it has not been allowed to season properly and will split as it dries.

Carved wooden masks are prominent among arts and crafts available in Jamaica.

There is also an amazing range of jewelry made from local products and semiprecious stones. These are extremely pretty and inexpensive, but you should be aware that some of the materials used are from protected species. Both tortoiseshell and coral are still on sale. Don't buy them. Not only is it illegal to import these articles back into your home country, but it encourages traders to take more of these endangered living creatures from the sea. Some traders will tell you that the coral jewelry or tortoiseshell they are selling was not taken from the sea but was washed up on the beaches; this is just a sales ploy.

You will also find a wide variety of basketware made locally from the rushes that can be found in huge beds all around the island. The dried-rush baskets are still used in many households today, and they make a very practical souvenir of your visit to Jamaica.

If you want to spend a bit more money on handcrafted goods, there are a number of galleries around the island where you can buy paintings and ceramics by some of the leading artists in Jamaica and the wider Caribbean. Harmony Hall at Ocho Rios is one, and the Half Moon Shopping Centre (just east of Montego Bay) also has a gallery. If you find yourself in Port Antonio, St. George Village has a number of studios featuring works of modern artists. To see crafts being made, tour the Wassi Art Pottery Factory near Ocho Rios (tel: 974-5044).

Clothing. Cool clothing remains a popular choice for shoppers, and Jamaica offers a wide range from designer wear in the boutiques of Kingston to the practical batik sarongs and T-shirts sold in beach stalls. If you travel light, you can buy your holiday wardrobe when you reach the island.

Coffee. Blue Mountain coffee can be bought and taken home in a number of forms. The roasted beans are sold in small sacks or in vacuum-packed foil containers. The beans can also be ground and then packed in tins or foil packs. Presentation packs (pretty printed bags) add an attractive exterior to the delicious contents.

Rum. The drink that sustained a thousand pirates and generations of the local people, Jamaican rum is said to be the best in the Caribbean —although other islands may beg to differ. Try before you buy. Appleton Distillery in St. Elizabeth offers a free tasting session as part of its tour (tel: 963-9215), including some of the mixed-rum drinks that are less alcoholic but equally delicious (see page 106). All these products are available throughout the island and at duty-free shops in the airport terminals.

Cocktails for two—rum provides the punch for most mixed drinks in Jamaica.

Cigars. For over 40 years, Jamaica has had a small-scale industry that produces a range of well-regarded cigars. These can be bought duty-free to take home with you. However, Cuban cigars are also a major business here. Jamaica is only 90 miles from the south coast of Cuba and imports a full range of what are reputed to be the finest cigars in the world, though they cannot be brought legally back to the US.

Duty-free shopping. The major resort towns all have duty-free shopping centers with a range of jewelry, perfume, leather goods, and other quality products from around the world. Here, items can be purchased with savings up to 30

An excursion on a glass-bottomed boat lets you view the sea life up-close in Negril.

percent on prices back home, but shopping is "buyer beware," since some products are not much better value than at your local department store. Do some research on prices before you travel if you want to be sure of making a saving.

ACTIVITIES FOR CHILDREN

Jamaica is an ideal island for children of all ages. There's nothing that young visitors like better than a beach and the sea; they can play for hours building sandcastles, swimming, or simply splashing in the water. Long Bay at Negril is perfect for young children, but all the major resorts have clean, safe beaches with good facilities. For older children, the beach can still hold a fascination. Snorkeling or taking a ride on a glass-bottomed boat will definitely keep their attention. Jamaica is an ideal place for kids to learn a new sporting skill. This will depend on the age of your children, but there are facilities for lessons in diving, horse riding, and golf. And having their hair put in braids will give them a lasting reminder that they really are in Jamaica.

Most large hotel complexes will offer activities for children. Some even have a children's club where kids can go off with new friends to spend the whole day enjoying special games and outings. Conversely, you should also be aware that some hotels on Jamaica operate on an "adults-only" policy. Always research the facilities available at any hotel before you make a reservation.

For all outdoor activities, always remember to cover young skin with a high factor sun-protection product and to limit their time in the sun for the first few days. Also make sure that they are well supervised whenever they are near the water.

Fun Things to Do with the Kids

Black River. The cruise into the Great Morass will introduce you to crocodiles, which come so close you can almost shake hands with them (tel: 965-2513).

Boston Bay. Try some original jerk. You'll be guaranteed a warm welcome from the stall traders if you have children with you: they love little ones.

Dunn's River Falls. Excitement for children and adults alike, plus lots of water activities.

Kingston. Tell them stories about Henry Morgan and the cut-throat pirate gangs and then take them to Port Royal to let their imaginations run wild.

Montego Bay. Travel underwater in a submersible boat. Kids will be captivated by the sea life that lies so close to the shore (tel: 979-2281).

Rafting on the Martha Brae River. It's fun to float down the river. Rafts take one child under 12 with two adults; older children must travel on a separate raft (tel: 952-0889).

Rose Hall Great House. (East of Montego Bay) The ghostly happenings will fascinate children of all ages—just don't let them have nightmares! (tel: 953-2323).

EATING OUT

Jamaica is a large and fertile island. Fruits and vegetables grow in abundance on family farms, and the land is grazed by cattle, goats, and pigs. The clear Caribbean waters are full of edible fish as well as lobster, shrimp, and other tasty seafood. You will be offered an amazing variety of dishes and treats, all of it very fresh. As a result, the range of eating opportunities across the island is remarkable, from cheap street stalls to beach bars to fine restaurants offering international selections and "new Jamaican" cooking.

What to Eat

Jamaican Cuisine

Jamaican cooks have used these raw materials to create a wide range of dishes that has developed into a unique cuisine. The island's historical and ethnic heritage has contributed to the blend as the range of dishes has grown: it is a story of African cooking techniques and Indian spices meeting Caribbean ingredients. Jamaican food has a reputation for being spicy but, surprisingly, most of the dishes are tasty but not hot. The heat comes from a sauce found in a little bottle that is always on the table, allowing you to add as much spice as you like—or none at all. This hot sauce is manufactured on the island with a secret recipe based on "Scotch bonnet" pepper, one of the hottest in the world. A little goes an awfully long way, so start carefully and discover your personal taste level.

You will find tame versions of all Jamaican dishes on the menu at large hotels. Hotels will often have a night of Jamaican cuisine where you can sample a range of dishes along with some Jamaican entertainment.

Tropical ambience—you can enjoy beach-side dining on lobster and snapper and a whole lot more at most resorts.

Ackee and saltfish. This dish was once a staple food for the slaves and is now the official national dish of Jamaica. *Ackee,* which is native to Ghana in West Africa, is a vegetable now found in great abundance on Jamaica. The ackee is harvested only when it is ripe, as it is poisonous otherwise. It is chopped and cooked until it takes on the appearance of firm scrambled eggs. The slaves added a small amount of protein-rich salted codfish for a cheap and nutritious way to start the day. Today ackee is often served with other types of fish or with bacon as part of a traditional Jamaican breakfast. It comes with various kinds of carbohydrate such as dumplings called "Johnny cakes," or perhaps with *bammy*, a cassava pancake.

Meat dishes. Jamaicans always cook their meat well rather than rare, so you won't have to worry about the dangers of undercooked meat. But meat served in local restaurants is chopped into pieces with a cleaver rather than being butchered and trimmed, so beware of sharp pieces of bone which might be present in the prepared dish.

Jerk. The modern national dish of Jamaica is "jerk," which takes its name from the hot marinade used to season meats or fish. You will find it everywhere from the menus of fine restaurants to beach bars and street barbecue stalls. The dish was invented in Maroon country (near Boston Bay in the east of the island) and was originally used to tenderize pork, which was then cooked slowly and served hot and tender. The marinade became popular across the island for all meat, and today you can eat jerk chicken and even jerk fish. The Boston recipe is a mixture of 21 spices and very piquant indeed.

You can watch jerk pork and chicken being prepared in Boston Bay and then try it for yourself. The meat is freshly butchered (the animals are slaughtered in the mornings under the auspices of health inspectors), then marinated and cooked within hours. You will be served the meat with breadfruit, which has a neutral flavor to cool the palate. In other parts of the island, the jerk ranges in flavor and hotness. In hotels and international restaurants, it can be quite mild; you'll find that Jamaicans snub their noses at such offerings.

Goat curry. There are herds of goats on all the highways and byways of Jamaica. Goat curry (referred to as "curry goat") became part of the Jamaican diet following the arrival of the Indian itinerant workers who came to work the plantations following the abolition of slavery. The curry style has adapted over the generations and is now really more of a flavor than a true Indian method of preparation.

Fish dishes. A most amazing array of fish and shellfish can be found in the waters surrounding Jamaica. You can be guaranteed absolutely fresh seafood because the small boats come in daily with their catch. In many restaurants the "catch of the day" will be the tastiest and freshest option. It might be tuna, snapper, or kingfish; whatever the choice, it will always be superb. The lobster and conch are also fresh and delicious, although they are seasonal. Different areas of the island specialize in certain types of seafood. Around Bluefields, south of Negril, it is spicy shrimp, and at Middle Quarter you will find Escovitch fish, which is fried and then pickled.

Rice and peas. Most main dishes are accompanied by a side dish of rice and peas. It originated as an inexpensive and nutritious option in colonial times, when it could be served as a meal in itself when money was scarce. The "peas" (actually red or kidney beans) and the rice are cooked slowly together with a bit of coconut milk. You can substitute french fries if you are not too keen on rice.

"Get your lobster here!" A fresh lobster vendor walks the beach with his wares.

A riverside fruit vendor at Black River displays the many tropical delicacies that grow in abundance in Jamaica.

Vegetables and fruit. Because fresh vegetables in Jamaica are varied and plentiful, you will always be given a generous accompaniment with any main dish. The list includes *callaloo* (a spinach-like vegetable), yam, breadfruit, pumpkin, and potatoes.

You can sample the abundant fresh fruits from stalls in the street or from hawkers on the beach. Hotels will have a wonderful selection at breakfast or to finish a meal in the evening. Bananas are obviously popular, but you can also choose from guava, mango, papaya, pineapple, and coconut. There is in addition a range of unusual fruits found only in Jamaica. Look out for sweetsop and soursop (rough-skinned fruits, said to be aphrodisiacs and best made into a milky drink) along with the star apple and the *ugli* (a citrus fruit).

The banana has a particular place in Jamaican cuisine, as befits its status as one of the island's major crops. It is eaten raw but also used in many hot desserts. You can have bananas in fritters and, for a real touch of luxury, flambéed in Jamaican rum.

Other hot and cold desserts come in the form of tarts and custards, traditionally flavored with coconut cream, which has a thick consistency and a sweet taste. Ice-cream made with fresh fruit are also extremely refreshing: "matrimony" is a Jamaican favorite and mixes orange and star apples with cream.

Snacks. Jamaican fast food consists of a number of cheap dishes that are prepared at home or bought at roadside stalls for lunch on the run. "Patties" are thin oven-baked pastries filled with meat, fish or vegetables. "Stamp-and-go" are fish fritters, so called because just before being cooked they are flattened with the palm of the hand. These dishes are often served as hors d'oeuvres in hotels or in private homes.

International Cuisine

In addition to serving toned-down versions of local dishes, Jamaica's resorts offer a wide range of international cuisine. There are a number of Italian restaurants all across the island, from those offering quick trattoria-style service to upscale dining establishments with full service. Visitors seeking Mexican and Chinese cooking will find choices as well, and the comforts of American and Continental food are also available. There are even branches of international fast food chains in Montego Bay and Ocho Rios if you want a burger or fried chicken.

What to Drink

One advantage of a trip to Jamaica compared to some other islands is that you can drink the tap water. You can be assured that food washed in tap water is safe to eat and that ice made from tap water is safe in your sodas or frozen daiquiris.

Beer. Red Stripe, a lager-type beer, has long been associated with Jamaica. It is light and very refreshing on a long, hot Jamaican day. You will find it in every café and bar. However, Jamaicans also have a liking for stout beers, which they like to drink at room temperature. You will find that Dragon Stout and Guinness are widely available. You can order your drink cold if you don't mind the locals having a little joke at your expense.

Rum. The first thing that you will be offered when you arrive at your hotel is a rum cocktail. Appleton, the "overproof" white rum, is the best-known brand, used as the basis for almost limitless recipes. Whichever rum you choose, be careful because they all "pack a punch." Many hotels and bars will have their own special recipes, but most will combine rum with fresh fruit juice, lime, or coconut milk. Rum can also be combined with cream and other flavorings to produce a range of smooth after-dinner drinks. Perhaps the best known liqueur is Tia Maria (produced from the Jamaican coffee bean), which makes the perfect accompaniment to a hot cup of coffee.

Non-alcoholic drinks. The choice of fruit juices is huge, and you can find single juices or blends in every bar and restaurant. "Ting," a refreshing fizzy grapefruit drink, is locally produced. Jamaica also produces a ginger ale which has a little more kick than the standard and is extremely refreshing in the heat of the day. You will find all the internationally recognized brands of soda readily available.

Beer or Policemen?

You might hear locals (particularly older Jamaicans) asking for a "policeman" when they enter a bar. Don't be alarmed by this—there isn't an emergency. They are merely asking for a Red Stripe beer. The name was taken from the stripes on the trousers and cap of the Jamaican police uniform.

Shake it, baby! A barman whips up a refreshing cocktail for beach revelers at Dragon Bay.

Jamaican coffee. Said to be the best in the world and extremely expensive due to the small crop and high demand, most Blue Mountain coffee is exported. You might not find it in every establishment on the island. The coffee is extremely mild and low in caffeine, with a hint of natural sweetness.

During the 1960s the reputation of Blue Mountain coffee suffered because inferior lowland beans began to be blended with quality mountain beans to increase the crop and meet demand. In 1973 the government stepped in to create an official standard for Blue Mountain coffee, thus restoring confidence in the marketplace. Today, only coffee produced at four estates can be sold as 100 percent Blue Mountain: Mavis Bank, Silver Hill, Moy Hall, and Wallenford. You might also discover products advertised as "blended" Blue Mountain coffee; these will contain at least 20 percent Blue Mountain beans.

HANDY TRAVEL TIPS

An A–Z Summary of Practical Information

ACCOMMODATION

Jamaica has a full range of accommodation, from basic beach shacks to luxury all-inclusive hotels, but it specializes in high-quality "get away from it all" paradise resorts. There are a number of options for room and meal plans.

AI All-Inclusive, with all sporting facilities, resort activities, meals, and drinks included in the room price.

AP American Plan, with all three meals included in the room price.

MAP Modified American Plan, with breakfast and dinner included in the room price.

BB Bed and Breakfast, basic room with a Jamaican breakfast.

EP European Plan, which is the price for the room only, without meals.

The Jamaica Tourist Board produces a comprehensive information sheet with hotel details and prices. It also operates a toll-free direct reservation service in the US at 800-526-2422 and in Canada at 800-432-7559.

Many large resorts offer such sporting facilities as golf courses, equestrian centers, scuba-diving lessons, and guided dives. They also offer wedding packages and honeymoon specials ranging in quality and price. Although All-Inclusive hotels offer all facilities for one price, it is important to check the quality of the facilities offered in each resort, as these do vary. Some AI packages still apply extra charges to certain activities or for "luxury" foods and premium brand alcohol.

Jamaica also has a range of private villas for rent, with or without staff. Contact the Jamaican Association of Villas and Apartments (JAVA), Pineapple Place, Ocho Rios (tel: 974-2508) for more details.

Prices change dramatically between high and low season. Low season is mid-April through mid-December, and you can make savings of up to 40 percent during this period. High season is extremely busy, so it is important to make reservations to guarantee the accommodation of your choice.

AIRPORTS (see also GETTING THERE)

There are two international airports on the island: Norman Manley International Airport at Kingston and Sangster International Airport at Montego Bay. Manley serves Kingston and the east of the island; it also caters to international business travelers. Sangster International serves the west of the island and also handles the charter aircraft that fly to the island.

A trip from Norman Manley Airport to downtown Kingston takes 20 minutes and is 15 km (9½ miles). There is a bus service, but a taxi direct to your destination is a more sensible option. Transfer time to Port Antonio is around 2 hours.

Downtown Montego Bay is only 5 minutes from Sangster International Airport, and there are ample taxis outside the terminal building even though many hotels and resorts will provide transport for the short transfer. Transfers to other resorts by coach are as follows: Ocho Rios is around 2 hours, Runaway Bay 1½ hours, and Negril 2 hours.

There are also a number of domestic airports: Negril Aerodrome, Boscobel (near Ocho Rios), Ken Jones Airport (Port Antonio), and Tinson Pen (Kingston), which all operate transfer flights from the two international airports.

B

BICYCLE RENTAL/HIRE

Bicycle rental is a sensible way to see a little more of the area where you are based. It is particularly useful in Negril, where the land is long and flat. It is also possible to undertake bicycle tours into the Blue Mountains and around Port Antonio, along the relatively quiet roads. Contact Blue Mountain Bicycle Tours on Main Street in Ocho Rios (tel: 974-7075; fax: 974-0635) or, in Negril, Dependable Bike Rental (tel: 957-4764). Cycles can be rented by the day or by the week.

BUDGETING for YOUR TRIP

Jamaica as a destination is a good value. To help you budget for your trip, here are some prices for the things you will need.

Accommodation. A room can range in price from US$40 to US$350 per night, depending on whether you opt for room only (EP) or for a fully inclusive luxury resort hotel (AI). Here are some general guidelines: For a room in a less expensive hotel, allow US$40–$70 per person; for a medium-standard hotel, prices range from US$100–$180 per night. All-Inclusive resorts start at over US$200 per day but can rise to more then US$350, depending on the facilities and comfort level provided.

Self catering. Houses with fully fitted kitchens and maid can start at around US$1,500 per week, and the very luxurious (such as those at Blue Lagoon) are US$4,000 per week. These prices can prove to be a good value on a per-person basis.

Meals. For lunch in a moderately priced but good establishment allow US$20 per person plus drinks; for dinner, allow US$40 per person plus drinks. Prices can be cheaper at beach bars or more expensive in first-class restaurants.

Car rental. Allow around US$70–$100 per day for a medium-sized car. The lower figure is the price in low season. Hiring a car with driver for a full-day tour will cost between US$80 and $100, which should include lunch.

Leaving the island. A departure tax of US$27 (J$1,000) should be included in the cost of the ticket, otherwise payment to be made in cash.

CAMPING

Camping is not a recommended form of accommodation in Jamaica.

CAR RENTAL

Jamaica is the third-largest of the Caribbean islands, and to see all its delights it is best to hire a car. However, the condition of the roads and Jamaican driving habits do create concerns (see Driving). With common sense and care, renting a car should enhance your trip, not spoil it.

The major car rental companies have offices at the two international airports:

Hertz: Kingston (tel: 924-8028), Montego Bay (tel: 979-0438). Head office can be reached at 952-4250 or 952-5200.

Avis: Kingston (tel: 926-1560), Montego Bay (tel: 952-2362).

Island Car Rental is the largest local fleet: Kingston (tel: 924-8075), Montego Bay (tel: 952-5771), Ocho Rios (tel: 974-2666).

Car hire is expensive in Jamaica, at an average of about US$90 per day, but prices drop in low season (mid-April through mid-December) to US$60 for a standard-size car. The international companies are more expensive than local companies but can offer newer and better maintained cars. Be aware that many rental agencies offer "new" cars that are two or three years old. Always satisfy yourself as to the age and condition of the car before confirming the booking. You can specify whether you want a manual or automatic transmission when making your booking. Many companies make an extra charge for delivering the car to your hotel; this can amount to another day's rental fee.

All national driving licenses will be recognized by rental companies. Drivers must have held a license for at least one year. All renters must post a deposit, which ranges from US$500 to $1000; if you are under 25 years of age, there will also be a bond to comply with insurance regulations. A credit card imprint will be the most sensible method of posting the deposit, although cash can also be used.

In the US, some insurance companies cover hire cars; check to see whether you are covered on your policy or through your credit card before purchasing insurance. Damage waiver is recommended, which will add around US$15 per day to your costs.

In high season it is important to book a car in advance, as demand will be high. In low season you should be able to negotiate a package that will give you a better price, and it can often be better to wait rather than book in advance.

Service stations are open daily and accept cash only (Jamaican dollars or American dollars) for fuel.

CLIMATE

Jamaica is a tropical island. It has virtually no change in seasons, the temperature varying between 25°C and 28°C (77°F and 83°F), although it is cooler in the mountains. Rainfall averages around 198 cm (78 inches) each year and is greatest between August and November, which is considered low season for visitors. However, rain can fall in short and heavy tropical showers at all times of the year, especially in the afternoon. Rainfall varies considerably between the wetter east and the drier west of the island. Hurricane season, which afflicts the whole Caribbean, runs from the beginning of June through the end of November.

Average daily temperatures for Jamaica:

	J	F	M	A	M	J	J	A	S	O	N	D
°C	25	25	25	26	27	28	28	28	28	27	26	25
°F	77	77	77	79	81	83	83	83	83	81	79	77

CLOTHING

Lightweight clothing is sensible throughout the year along the coasts. Many people manage happily with T-shirts and shorts during the day, something a little more formal in the evening. Cotton or the new breathable materials are ideal. In the mountains, sweaters are a good idea for evenings or in case of a change in the weather. If you plan to visit interior towns or Kingston, more conservative clothing might be appropriate. Beachwear is acceptable only in the immediate area of the beach.

A hat and sunglasses are important, as the sun is very strong, especially in the middle of the day. When you first arrive, always make sure that you have clothing to cover your skin to prevent burning; a lightweight long-sleeved shirt is fine.

Footwear should be light and comfortable: a pair of sandals or flip-flops for the beach, along with a smarter choice for evenings. If you plan to visit the Blue Mountains, a pair of stout shoes or walking boots would be useful.

COMPLAINTS

Complaints should always be addressed initially to the individual, hotel, restaurant, or organization involved. If the complaint cannot be amicably resolved, take your problem to the Jamaica Tourist Board for further assistance.

CRIME and SAFETY

Jamaica and, Kingston in particular, have a reputation for crime and violence, however the picture that has been painted in the media does not do the island or its capital city justice. The Jamaican countryside has a comparatively low crime rate. Much of the violent crime is confined to about four police districts in Kingston, which are prone to drug and political inter-neighborhood rivalry. As with any city, visitors are advised to exercise caution.

The use of marijuana, or "ganja" (as it is known on the island), is not uncommon among Jamaicans of all classes, many smoke it, while others use it as a medicinal herb. Rastafarians use it as a sacrament in religious observances. The drug is easily available and most visitors will be offered a supply at some stage during their holiday. But whatever the supposed merits of the drug, Jamaican law is very clear: It is strictly illegal to possess or use marijuana, and punishments are severe for those who are caught.

For other forms of crime, simply take the same precautions you would observe in any other destination. Do not wear expensive jewelry or leave your possessions lying around in public places. Do not carry large amounts of cash. Take traveler's checks instead of cash; these offer more protection because you can obtain replacements if they are stolen. Always leave things that you don't need locked in your room safety deposit box, and keep all valuables in the hotel safe.

Don't walk into unlit areas after dark and don't get into a car with someone that you don't know.

The Jamaican authorities have increased security patrols in the resort areas, and you will see the blue uniforms of the "Tourist Police" on the beaches. Many hotels also employ private security personnel, who patrol beaches and hotel entrances to deter hawkers and others.

Many Jamaican men make a living as impromptu (and definitely unofficial) guides, and they might approach you in the street or on the beach. Use caution in your dealings and use accredited companies only. Do not accept offers to ride in unauthorized taxis (official taxis have red license plates); they will not be insured to carry fare-paying passengers.

Always take out insurance to cover loss, theft, illness, and accident when traveling abroad. Always keep a separate listing of passport numbers, insurance policy numbers, driver's license numbers, and similar important documents just in case you need to make a claim. Photocopying important documents is an even better protection plan.

CUSTOMS and ENTRY REQUIREMENTS

Residents of the US and from most Commonwealth and European countries do not need a visa to visit Jamaica. Visitors from the US and Canada can enter with a valid passport, naturalization certificate, or photo I.D. with birth certificate. British and other European citizens must have a valid passport valid for six months and a return ticket. Visitors from Australia and New Zealand need valid passports.

No vaccinations are required unless you have visited the following areas within six weeks before your visit to Jamaica: Asia, Africa, Central and South America, Dominican Republic, Haiti, and Trinidad and Tobago. Please contact the Tourist Information Board for further advice if you have traveled to these destinations.

Items that may be brought into Jamaica duty-free are 1 quart of liquor (except rum) and 1 pound of tobacco in any form. Restricted items include certain types of fresh goods (flowers, plants, honey, fruits, vegetables) and coffee. Strictly prohibited are firearms, explosives, and dangerous drugs. Kosher foods may be brought into Jamaica but require special documentation.

You should declare any unusual or expensive items (such as cameras or electrical goods) on arrival to assure the authorities that they are for personal use only.

DRIVING

Driving in Jamaica is an adventure or a worry, depending on your point of view. The roads are in very bad condition, particularly around the resort areas, where there is an awful lot of traffic. You might find cars driving toward you on the wrong side of the road, only to realize that they are avoiding a large pothole on their own side of the street. Always drive with utmost care and be ready to stop at any moment for potholes, animals, and people. Cross-country routes, particularly in the area of the Blue Mountains, are prone to flooding or landslides. After periods of rain, you should always check before setting out to be sure that the road is passable; ask bus or truck drivers or employees at your hotel.

Speed limits and safety. Vehicles drive on the left side of the road, and speed limits are 50 km/h (30 mph) in towns and 80 km/h (50 mph) in rural areas. Despite this, many Jamaican drivers ignore the speed limits and drive at a dangerous speed. Always drive at a safe pace and allow plenty of time to reach your destination. Roundabouts or traffic circles are common. Give way to any traffic from the right that is already in the traffic circle.

Road signs feature easily recognizable international symbols. However, you will find that distance signs can be in either miles or kilometers, which can create confusion. The unit of measurement used will always be indicated at the side of the number. The area around Treasure Beach (in the south) is not well posted with signs, so patience and good map-reading skills will be useful there.

Many Jamaicans do not own vehicles, so offering lifts to neighbors is normal. Pedestrians might raise a hand for a lift as you pass, especially in country areas. Many vehicles will stop suddenly or will not signal before they pull off the road to pick up passengers. When driving in Jamaica, you should not pick up passengers.

Fuel and service. There are fuel stations open seven days a week in all towns. Fuel is paid for in cash only, although this can be in US as well as Jamaican dollars. Always carry out basic checks on a rental vehicle when you take delivery of it and before setting out. Public telephones are rare in the interior; if you do break down, it could be hours before you get help, unless you rent a cellular phone. If you have mechanical difficulties, contact your rental company for assistance.

Fluid measures

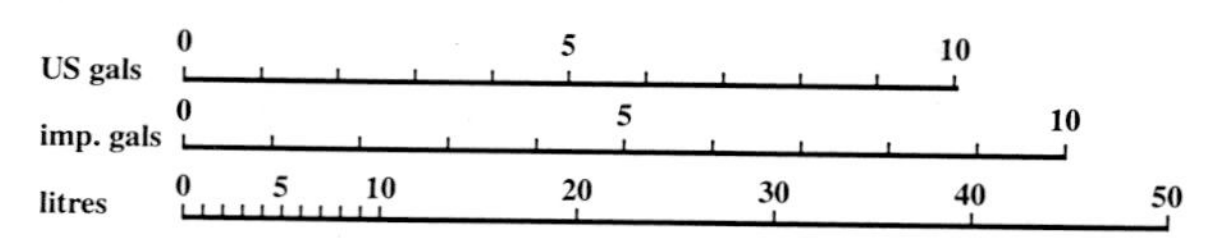

Distance

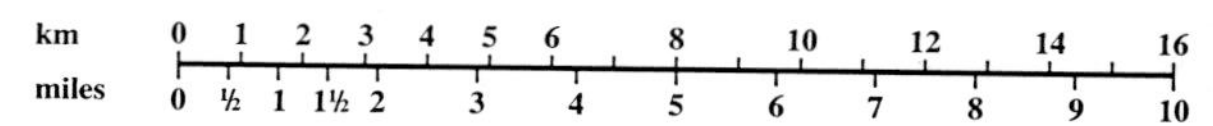

Parking. When parking in towns or near beaches, try to find a car park with some security, and always park with the car in full view. At night, always park in a well-lit location. Never leave anything of value in your car, and put all other items out of sight in the trunk.

E

ELECTRIC CURRENT

Jamaica operates at 110 volts/50 cycles as standard; current at 220 volts is available in some hotels on the island. Appliances with US and Canadian plugs can be used without adapters.

EMBASSIES, CONSULATES, and HIGH COMMISSIONS

All diplomatic representatives have offices in Kingston.

Australian High Commission: 64 Knutsford Boulevard, Kingston 5, tel: 926-3550.

British High Commission: 26 Trafalgar Road, Kingston 10, tel: 510-0700, 926-1022/3 (visa enquiries).

Canadian High Commission: 3 West Kings House Road, Waterloo Road Entrance, Kingston 5, tel: 926-1500.

US Embassy: Jamaica Mutual Life Centre, 2 Oxford Street, Kingston 5, tel: 929-4850; fax: 926-6743.

New Zealand citizens should contact the Australian High Commission in case of difficulty.

Irish citizens should contact the British High Commission.

EMERGENCIES

In the event of an emergency, call 911 for police and 110 for fire or ambulance services.

G

GAY and LESBIAN TRAVELERS

Homosexuality is an offence, punishable by prison in Jamaica. Consequently, homophobia is rife and there is no open gay "scene".

GETTING THERE (see also AIRPORTS)

By air. Flying into Jamaica is an easy option from the US, Canada, and Europe. Miami, New York, Atlanta, Chicago, and Toronto are all major hubs in North America, with easy connections to other US and Canadian cities. London is the hub for Europe, with easy connections for the UK and Ireland. The following major airlines fly into Jamaica: Air Jamaica, Air Canada, American Airlines, British Airways, Northwest Airlines, and US Air. Scheduled flights will normally land at Norman Manley International Airport in Kingston. If you will be spending most of your time around Montego Bay or Negril, it would be much more convenient to land at Sangster International Airport at Montego Bay, where the transfer time is much shorter.

Many other scheduled airlines and charter companies offer service depending on the time of year, with more service during high season. Most charter flights land at Montego Bay in the north. Consult a travel agent for the most appropriate service for your plans.

Visitors from Australia and New Zealand can travel through either the US or Britain to pick up a connection to Jamaica. Both directions involve long journeys and possibly a stopover en route, so consult an airline specialist for advice about schedules and costs.

By sea. Many tourists visit Jamaica as a port-of-call on a cruise. Montego Bay and Ocho Rios are major cruise destinations, with comprehensive facilities for cruise passengers. Both ports are well placed to offer tours to a range of attractions that can be visited on your day ashore. Cruise companies all offer different packages with different prices; individual ships belonging to the same company have different facilities and levels of comfort and luxury. Before booking, research what is available on board as thoroughly as you would a hotel on land to avoid having a disappointing trip.

GUIDES and TOURS

There is a very comprehensive tour program offering visits to sites across the island. These can be booked either through your own tour or cruise company or through the Tourist Board offices. For those who don't want to hire a car, this is an ideal way to see more of Jamaica. Tour companies will pick you up at your hotel and bring you back at the end of the day. Full-day tours often include lunch.

JUTA (Jamaican Union of Travelers Association), the major agency, provides licensed taxis and tour buses for excursions to all major attractions (tel: 968-7088; fax: 974-9124); there are JUTA branches around the island. JUTA can also arrange individual itineraries.

Prices for the same tour do vary, and you can save money by booking directly with JUTA or with the Jamaica Tourist Board, rather than through your own tour operator.

H

HEALTH and MEDICAL CARE

For medical emergencies, phone 110.

Hygiene standards are generally high on Jamaica, and the tap water is drinkable. There are some minor nuisances that can be avoided. Mosquitoes can be a problem, especially just after sunset, so cover up or apply insect repellent. Don't step on the spiny sea urchins as you snorkel or dive; the spines will imbed themselves into your flesh and the sores can become infected. Go easy on the alcohol, especially in the sunshine, as this can lead to dehydration. Take time to build a tan to avoid sunburn and sunstroke; use a sunscreen with a sufficiently high SPF (Sunscreen Protection Factor). If you are already taking medication, it would be sensible to anticipate your needs for the trip, as pharmacies here are less well stocked than at home.

Most hotels have an arrangement with a local doctor who will be on-call for any problem. Each major town on the island has a hospital; however, the nearest hospital to Ocho Rios is at St. Ann's Bay, and the closest to Negril is at Savanna-la-Mar.

Always take out comprehensive insurance when you travel to cover unforeseen health emergencies or accidents.

HITCHHIKING

On an island where many families do not own transport (particularly in rural areas), you will find many local people asking for and offering lifts. However, local people are not accustomed to tourists asking for lifts, and hitchhiking in Jamaica carries the same risks as in any other destination.

LANGUAGE

English is the official language of Jamaica and is spoken by everyone on the island. However, the local population also uses a Caribbean-English creole language when speaking with each other.

It originally developed when the Elizabethan English of the British colonists mixed with the West African languages spoken by slaves. With subsequent additions of English, African, and Spanish vocabulary, Jamaican English has evolved into an everyday medium that is difficult for outsiders to understand.

LAUNDRY and DRY CLEANING

All major hotels offer reliable laundry service. You will find private laundries in the major towns, but services are not of a uniform standard and can take time.

M

MAPS

The Jamaica Tourist Board publishes a "Discover Jamaica" road map, which includes town maps of Kingston, Negril, Mandeville, Montego Bay, Spanish Town, Ocho Rios, and Port Antonio. Unfortunately, it has not been updated for several years.

MEDIA

Radio and television. Jamaica has three TV stations and ten radio stations, some of which are owned by the government. There are also a number of independent local radio stations, each of which operates only in a limited area. Most hotels and many bars also receive US satellite services, so you'll find CNN and ESPN widely available.

Newspapers and magazines. The major daily national newspapers in Jamaica are the *Daily Gleaner* and the *Jamaica Observer*, alongside *The Star*, a daily tabloid, and the *Sunday Herald*, a national weekly. All newspapers can be bought at newsagents or from roadside vendors in towns. Foreign newspapers and magazines can be found in larger hotels, at the airports, and at some duty-free shops in the major resort areas.

MONEY MATTERS

Currency. The currency of Jamaica is the Jamaican dollar (colloquially called the "jay"), and there are 100 cents in each dollar. Paper bills are issued in denominations of $1, $2, $20, $50, $100 and $500; coins are issued in denominations of 10 cents, 20 cents, 50 cents, $1, and $5. The smaller coins, being practically worthless, are being phased out. The US dollar is also widely accepted in shops and restaurants.

Jamaican dollars may be converted to foreign currency at the airport before departing for home upon the presentation of an official exchange receipt. If you intend to arrive or leave with more than US$10,000 or J$150,000, you must declare this to Jamaican Customs.

Traveler's checks and credit cards. Traveler's checks are widely accepted in Jamaica for cash in banks, for goods in shops, and for hotel and restaurant charges. Credit cards are also widely accepted except for fuel purchases, which must be made with cash (Jamaican or US dollars). If you want to obtain a cash advance with a credit card, you must take your card into a bank. Increasing numbers of Automatic Teller Machines (ATMs) in Jamaica accept international cards.

Currency exchange. Money is changed at hotels, though at a less advantageous rate than in banks. There are also a number of "Cambio" shops which are official money changers. You must have one official exchange receipt if you want to change money back before you return home. Changing money on the black market is illegal, but it is one of the services offered by street merchants. Beware of being cheated if you use these unofficial money changers.

OPENING HOURS

Banks. 9am–2pm Monday to Thursday; 9am–4pm Friday.
Business offices (including Tourist Board). 8:30am–4:30pm, Monday to Friday.

Shops. 9am–5pm Monday to Saturday, but this can vary enormously in resort towns and from low to high season.
Museums and galleries. 10am–5pm Monday to Saturday, but private "great houses" and plantations are open daily.

P

POLICE

Police officers wear navy uniforms with red stripes on the hat and trousers. The emergency phone number for the police is 119.

POST OFFICES

All major towns have a Post Office. These are open Monday through Friday 8am–5pm. The postal system is notoriously slow, and postcards often take three weeks to reach their destination. If you have anything important or urgent to send, use a commercial carrier.

PUBLIC HOLIDAYS

Government offices and services are generally closed on the following days:

New Year's Day (1 January)
Ash Wednesday
Good Friday
Easter Monday
Labour Day (23 May)
Emancipation Day (1 August)
Independence Day (6 August)
National Heroes Day (third Monday in October)
Christmas Day (25 December)
Boxing Day (26 December)

PUBLIC TRANSPORTATION

The metropolitan areas of Kingston and Montego Bay have an improved bus system. Taxis and bus franchises provide easy commuting to coastal and interior areas of the island.

The tour company JUTA operates commercial air-conditioned bus services between the airports and the major resort areas. As an example, a one-way trip from Sangster Airport at Montego Bay to Negril costs around US$20.

Once you are settled, many restaurants and bars will provide free transportation in the evenings if you eat with them; just give them a call from your hotel. Taxis are plentiful, but remember to use cars with red license plates: these are registered and properly insured. Always agree on a price for the ride before you get into the taxi, as they do not carry trip meters. Find out from other travelers what the going rate is for the journey that you want to make.

R

RELIGION

Jamaica is a Christian island, with Protestant denominations in the majority. However, many other major religions are also represented and have places of worship. Contact the Tourist Board for details about church services.

One of the significant religious minorities is the Rastafarian movement, whose true adherents are said to number fewer than 100,000. With their characteristic dreadlocked hair, they are seen as being almost synonymous with the image of Jamaica. Their influence on the popular culture of the island remains strong.

T

TELEPHONE

Emergency numbers in Jamaica: Police 119, Fire/Ambulance 110.

Local calls. When in Jamaica, you need dial only the seven-digit local number; there are no area codes within Jamaica.

There is a network of public telephones on Jamaica. All the smaller settlements rely on them as a means of communication. Many public phones, especially in the resort areas, take phone cards; others only take coins. Phone cards are available from hotels, banks, and shops. Coin-operated phones will take money after the connection has been made.

The fully digital direct-dial system on the island is prone to glitches. Many larger hotels will have direct-dial but will charge a premium for calls made. Smaller hotels will allow calls from the reception telephone but will also charge a premium for the service.

Long distance. When calling from abroad, the country code for Jamaica is 876. When making an international call from Jamaica, always dial 00 before the country code. Some frequently dialed international codes are as follows: US 1, Canada 1, UK 44, Ireland 353, South Africa 27, New Zealand 64, Australia 61.

TIME ZONES

Jamaica operates on Eastern Standard Time, which is 5 hours behind GMT; however, it does not switch to daylight saving time. The following chart shows the time in various cities in winter:

Los Angeles	New York	Jamaica	London	Sydney
9am	noon	noon	5pm	4am (next day)

TIPPING

Tipping is standard practice throughout the island, except at a few all-inclusive resorts where the "no tipping" policy is clearly stated. It is becoming more common for a service charge to be automatically added to restaurant bills; this should be clearly stated on the menu or on the bill. If not, then a 10 percent to 15 percent tip should be added.

For taxi drivers, tip 10 percent to 15 percent; for porters, J$10 per bag; for hotel maids, J$100 per day.

TOILETS/RESTROOMS

There are very few public toilets on Jamaica. Use toilets in hotels and restaurants or at attractions before setting out on journeys.

TOURIST INFORMATION OFFICES

For useful information to help you plan your trip, the Jamaica Tourist Board has offices in the following cities:

US: 1-800-233-4582 (toll-free). Offices are in *Chicago* at 500 N Michigan Avenue, Suite 1030, Chicago IL 60611, tel: (312) 527-1296; in *Los Angeles* at 3440 Wilshire Boulevard, Suite 805, Los Angeles CA 90010, tel: (213) 384-1123; in *Miami* at 1320 South Dixie Highway, Suite 1101, Coral Gables FL 33146, tel: (305) 665-0557; fax: (305) 666-7239; in *New York City* at 801 Second Avenue, 20th Floor, New York NY 10017, tel: (212) 856-9727; fax: (212) 856-9730.

UK: 1-2 Prince Consort Road, London SW7 2BZ, England, tel: (020) 7224-0505; fax: (020) 7224-0551.

Canada: 303 Eglinton Avenue East, Suite 200, Toronto, Ontario M4P 1L3, tel: (416) 482-7850; fax: (416) 482-1730; 1-800-465-2624 (toll free).

In Jamaica: There are several ways to obtain tourist information when you are on the island. The Tourist Information Helpline is toll-free at the following numbers: 888-991-4400 or 888-991-9999. Tourist Offices can be found in the following locations: in *Kingston* at 64 Knutsford Boulevard, P.O. Box 360, Kingston 5 (tel: 929-9200); at *Norman Manley International Airport* (tel: 924-8023/4; fax 929-9375); on the *south coast* in the Hendriks Building, 2 High Street, Black River, St. Elizabeth (tel: 965-2074; fax: 965-2076); in *Montego Bay* at Cornwall Beach, P.O. Box 67, Gloucester Avenue, Montego Bay; at *Sangster International Airport* (tel: 952-4427/8); in *Negril* at Coral Seas Plaza, Negril (tel: 957-4243; fax: 957-4489); in *Ocho Rios* at Ocean Village Shopping Centre, P.O. Box 240, Ocho Rios (tel: 974-2582/3, or 974-2570; fax: 974-2559); and in *Port Antonio* at City Centre Plaza, P.O. Box 151, Port Antonio (tel: 993-3051 or 993-2587; fax: 993-2117).

Planning your trip on the Web. A number of websites can provide you with information about Jamaica before you book your trip, including details about hotels and attractions, car rental companies, and general facts and history:

<www.visitjamaica.com> official site of the Jamaica Tourist Board

<www.jamaica.com> good links

<www.negril.com/beingee2.htm>

<www.whatsonjamaica.com> weekly entertainment and sport guide

All these sites will link you with other useful sites for your trip. In addition, individual hotel websites and e-mail addresses have been added to the "Hotels and Restaurants" section at the end of this book.

WEIGHTS and MEASURES

Jamaica uses standard metric weights and measures.

Length

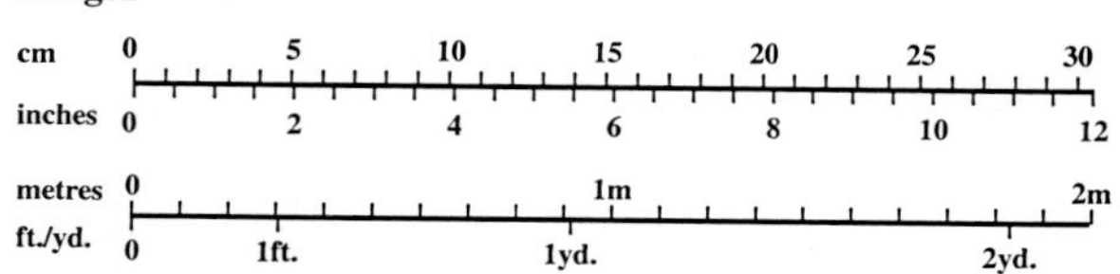

Weight

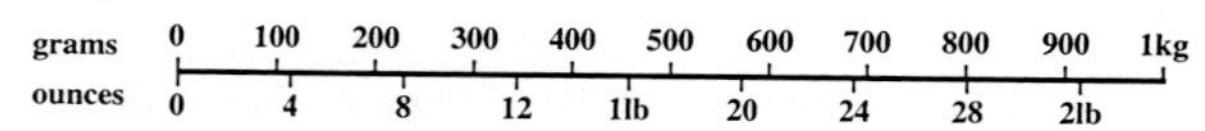

Temperature

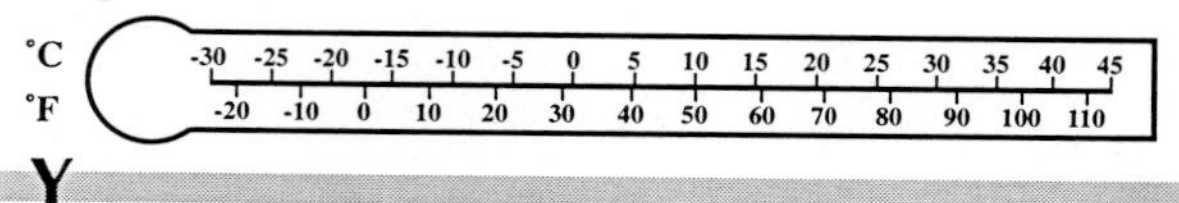

Y

YOUTH HOSTELS

There are no youth hostels in Jamaica.

Recommended Hotels

In both style and price, there is a wide choice of accommodation in Jamaica. At the upper end of the scale are very expensive, luxurious resort hotels as well as the "all-inclusive" resorts, where every service and facility (even meals) in the hotel is included in the price, which you pay when making a booking. There is also a range of standard hotels at all levels. More modest accommodation can be found in small guest-houses and family-run hotels that offer clean rooms but few other facilities. Some historic plantation houses have been converted into hotels for a "colonial feel." Many hotels welcome children and have special programs for them, but others are exclusively for adults. Whatever your budget and taste, there will be something on the island to suit you.

If you are booking by telephone or fax direct to Jamaica, be sure to dial the island's international code —which is 876 —before the hotel's seven-digit number.

The following selection of hotels covers the full spectrum of accommodation options. The categories below indicate prices in US dollars per room, based on double occupancy (except for the "All-Inclusive" hotels, marked "AI," whose rates include all meals, drinks, and sporting facilities).

$$$$$	over $200
$$$$	$140–$200
$$$	$90–$140
$$	$50–$90
$	under $50

Negril

Hedonism II $$$$$ *(AI) Norman Manley Blvd., P.O. Box 25, Negril, tel: 957-5200, 957-5204, 957-3660, 800-417-5288 (toll-free from US and Canada); fax: 957-5289; e-mail:*

<info@breezes.com>; website: <www.breezes.com>. An all-inclusive, "anything goes" swinging resort at the north end of the beach in 22 acres of landscaped gardens. Includes land and water sports and nightly entertainment. Tile floors, mirrored ceilings above the beds. 280 rooms. Major credit cards.

Negril Tree House Resort $$-$$$ *Norman Manley Boulevard, P.O. Box 29, Negril, tel: 957-4287, 957-4288, 957-3503/4, 800-NEGRIL (toll-free from US); fax: 957-4386; e-mail: <jacksonj@cwjamaica.com>.* Set centrally amid the hotspots of the beach with plenty of entertainment choices for both day and night. Comfortable beachside rooms with TVs and safety-deposit boxes. 70 rooms. Major credit cards.

Rockhouse Hotel $$$$ *West End, Negril, tel: 957-4373, 957-0485, 957-0557; fax: 957-4373; e-mail: <rock house@toj.com>; website: <www.rockhousehotel.com>.* Commanding a rocky promontory in West End with views of spectacular sunsets, this collection of thatch-roofed villas has a tranquil setting. Cliff-top pool and access to swimming and snorkeling in Pristine Cove more than make up for no sandy beach. Not suitable for young children. 28 rooms. Major credit cards.

Sandals Negril Beach Resort and Spa $$$$$ *(AI) Norman Manley Boulevard, P.O. Box 12, Negril, tel: 957-5216, 957-5201, 957-5254, 800-SANDALS (toll-free from US); fax: 957-5338; e-mail: <sng@toj.com>; website: <www.sandals.com>.* Luxurious yet laid-back, with a slightly wicked reputation, on a sought-after stretch of the beach. A couples only all-inclusive resort. Four restaurants ranging from Jamaican and Japanese to low-calorie, stir-fried specialties and international cuisine. 223 rooms. Major credit cards.

Couples Swept Away Negri $$$$$ *(AI) Norman Manley Boulevard, P.O. Box 77, Negril, tel: 957-4061, 957-4066, 957-3258, 957-3262, 957-6388, 800-545-7937 (toll-free from US);*

fax: 957-4060; e-mail: <info@couples.com>; website: <www.sweptaway.com>. Beachfront all-inclusive hotel for couples only. Sports and fitness complex and live entertainment. Five bars and two restaurants with good health-food selection. 134 rooms. Major credit cards.

Xtabi Resort $-$$$ *P.O. Box 19, Light House Road, West End, Negril, tel: 957-4336, 957-0524, 957-0827, 957-0121; fax: 957-0127; e-mail: <xtabiresort @toj.com>; website: <www.negril-jamaica.com>.* Seven sea-front cottages in tropical gardens on the cliffs. Steps lead down to caves for snorkeling. Native wood floors and rustic furnishings; outside showers with privacy walls. All rooms have safes, some have kitchenettes, and many have refrigerators; garden rooms more modern, with tiled floors and air-conditioning. 23 rooms. Major credit cards.

Montego Bay

Breezes Montego Bay $$$$$ *(AI) Gloucester Avenue, White Sands Post Office, Montego Bay, tel: 940-1150, 940-1157, 940-5552, 940-5765; fax: 940-1160; e-mail: <info@breezes.com>; website: <www.breezes.com>.* All-inclusive accommodations range from intimate cabins to lavish suites. All rooms are tiled, air-conditioned, and equipped with satellite TV, clock radio, telephone, safe-deposit box, and hair dryer. Dining facilities include Jimmy's Buffet and Martino's Italian restaurant; pool-side bar serves snacks throughout the day. Close to airport and Doctor's Cave Beach. 124 rooms. Major credit cards.

Coyaba Beach Resort and Club $$$$ *Lot 22 Mahoe Bay, Rose Hall, tel: 953-2681, 953-3394, 800-330-8272 (toll-free from US and Canada); fax: 953-2244; e-mail: <info@ changes.com>; website: <www.coyabajamaica.com>.* Plantation-style rooms with hand-carved furniture, satellite television, "silent" air conditioning, ceiling fans, hairdryers, in-room safes. Private white-sand beach, swimming pool, heated jacuzzi, and a private dock with pick-up for fishing and diving charters. Complimentary water sports including sailing, windsurfing, kayaking, pedal boats, and snorkeling. 50 rooms. Major credit cards.

Half Moon Golf, Tennis, and Beach Club $$$-$$$$ *Rose Hall, P.O. Box 80, Montego Bay, tel: 953-2211, 953-2615, 800-626-0592 (toll-free from US); fax: 953-2731; e-mail: <hmoon-vd@infochan.com>; website: <www.halfmoon.com.jm>.* Beautifully landscaped gardens and a private bay giving the resort its name. Mahogany furniture, Jamaican paintings, cable TV, air conditioning, mini-bars, hair dryers, and in-room safes. Asian-style restaurant, English pub, and a coffee shop. Land and water sports include squash, tennis, health and fitness center, equestrian center, and a par-72 championship golf course. 338 rooms. Major credit cards.

Round Hill Hotel and Villas $$$ *P.O. Box 64, Hopewell Post Office, Montego Bay, tel: 956-7050, 956-7055, 800-972-2159 (toll-free from US); fax: 956-7505; e-mail: <roundhill@cwjamaica.com>; website: <www.roundhilljamaica.com>.* A casually elegant hotel set in what was once a pineapple plantation, with seaside freshwater pool and opportunities for snorkeling in crystal clear waters of a private white-sand beach. Well-equipped exercise room; varied nightly entertainment including beach bonfire picnic with calypso tunes and dancing. 120 rooms. Major credit cards.

Sandals Montego Bay $$$$$ *(AI) P.O. Box 100, Kent Avenue, Montego Bay, tel: 952-5510, 979-3136, 979-3132; fax: 952-0816; e-mail: <info@sandals.com>; website: <www.sandals.com>.* Situated on its own private beach just ten minutes from the airport and seconds away from the coral reefs offshore. All-inclusive couples-only resort has rooms with king-sized beds, air conditioning, cable TV, clock radio, and coffee-making facilities. 245 rooms. Special equipment available for disabled guests. Major credit cards.

The Tryall Club $$$$$ *P.O. Box 1206, Montego Bay, tel: 956-5660, 800-742-0498, 956-5855, 956-5859 or 800-238-5290 (toll-free from US); fax: 956-5673; website: <www.tryall.com>.* A luxurious seaside villa hideaway with a championship golf course on a tropical estate originally built as a sugar plantation. Presided over by a 162-year-old Georgian-style great house and situated on manicured gardens and rolling hills, with a palm-dotted white sand beach. 69 rooms. Major credit cards.

Wyndham Rose Hall Golf and Beach Club $$$$ *Rose Hall, P.O. Box 999, Montego Bay, tel: 953-2650, 953-2654, 800-WYNDHAM (toll-free from US); fax: 518-0203, reservations fax: 518-0205.* Situated on an old sugar plantation and along a stretch of secluded, sandy beach. All rooms have color TV, alarm clock/radio, en-suite bathrooms, real hangers, and shower massage. Shopping arcade, beauty salon, and golf course. 489 rooms. Major credit cards.

Ocho Rios

Ciboney Ocho Rios $$$$$ *(AI) P.O. Box 728, Ocho Rios, tel: 974-0389, 974-1203, 974-1039, 800-CIBONEY (toll-free from US); fax: 974-5838; e-mail: <ciboney@infochan.com>.* All-inclusive units are in villas and a great house in tropical setting overlooking Caribbean. Water sports include snorkeling, sunfish sailing, windsurfing, kayaking, and glass-bottomed boat trips; also tennis, horseshoes, volleyball, basketball, and golf. Four restaurants and two cafés. 289 rooms. Major credit cards.

Hibiscus Lodge $$$ *83–87 Main Street, P.O. Box 52, Ocho Rios, tel: 974-2676, 974-2594, 974-6629; fax: 974-1874.* Rooms perched on top of cliffs surrounded by extensive gardens, with paths and stairways down to snorkeling opportunities. Glass-shuttered rooms with verandas offering views of the sea, located a short way out of the center of Ocho Rios. Good sized swimming pool and cliff-top jacuzzi. Selection of open and covered restaurants. 26 rooms. Major credit cards.

The Little Pub Hotel $$ *59 Main St., P.O. Box 256, Ocho Rios, tel: 974-2324, 974-5826, 974-6570; fax: 974-5825; e-mail: <littlepub@infochannel.com>; website: <www.smiley.be/littlepub>.* An unusual two-story Georgian building five minutes from the beach, centrally located in a lively complex of restaurants, cocktail bar with a resident band, and shops. All rooms with air-conditioning (some with loft) and cable TV. 25 rooms. Major credit cards.

Renaissance Jamaica Grande $$$$ *Main Street, P.O. Box 100, Ocho Rios, tel: 974-2201, 974-2219, 795-2833; fax: 974-2289; e-mail: <jagrande@mail.infochan.com>; website: <www. renaissancehotels.com>.* Beachfront location overlooking the cruise port, with three swimming pools, two whirlpools, water sports center, sauna, steam room, exercise and weight room, plus lighted tennis courts. Five restaurants. 720 rooms. Major credit cards.

Port Antonio

Blue Lagoon Villas $$$$ *P.O. Box 2, Fairy Hill, Port Antonio, tel: 993-8491, 800-337-3499 (toll-free from US); fax: 993-8492; e-mail: <austria@cwjamaica.com>; website: <www. portantonio.com/blmain.htm>.* Luxurious sophistication next to the Blue Lagoon. You can reach four white-sand beaches, four restaurants, five bars, and an island by taking a boat or simply diving from your villa's deck and swimming to them. 26 rooms. Major credit cards.

Couples $$$$$ *(AI) Tower Isle, P.O. Box 330, Ocho Rios, tel: 975-4271, 975-4275, 800-COUPLES (toll-free from US); fax: 975-4439; website: <www.couples.com>.* An all-inclusive beachfront resort for couples only. All rooms have either ocean or mountain view, air conditioning, balcony or patio, king-sized beds, satellite TV, compact disc/cassette players, and in-room safes. Tropical Mini-Jungle with two jacuzzis, private island for nude sunbathing, plus swim-up pool bar, hammocks, lounge chairs. 221 rooms. Major credit cards.

Dragon Bay Hotel $$$$ *Fairy Hill District, P.O. Box 176, Port Antonio, tel: 993-7119, 993-7485; fax: 993-3284; e-mail: <reservations@dragonbay.com>; website: <www.dragonbay.com>.* A secluded and tranquil setting in Dragon Bay. Colonial-style central building with pub, fitness room, and shops is surrounded by villas with views overlooking the bay. Each room is equipped with refrigerator, kettle, hair dryer, and coffee-making facilities. 30 villas (suites above, rooms below). Major credit cards.

Goblin Hill Villas at San San $$$$ *11 East Avenue, Kingston 10, tel: call collect 925-8108 or 925-7896, 800-472-1148 (toll-free from US); fax: 925-6248.* A lush site set high on a hillside with excellent views over the sea. Self-contained villas with fully equipped kitchens staffed with cook/housekeeper. Freshwater swimming pool and two tennis courts. Complimentary access to San San beach; nature trails lead through a rain-forest environment. 28 villas. Major credit cards.

Mocking Bird Hill Hotel $$$ *P.O. Box 254, Port Antonio, tel: 993-7267; fax: 993-7133; e-mail: <mockbrd@cwjamaica.com>.* A tranquil environment nestled in verdant foothills of the Blue Mountains, decorated throughout with original art. White-tiled rooms with Jamaican hand-crafted bamboo furniture and locally printed fabrics offer panoramic views. Fine restaurant. 10 rooms. Major credit cards.

Trident Villas and Hotel $$$$ *P.O. Box 119, Port Antonio, tel: 993-2602, 993-2705, 800-633-3284 (toll-free from US or Canada); fax: 993-2590, 993-2960, or (201) 767-5510; e-mail: <trident@infochan.com>.* Antique-furnished rooms on coastline gardens offer a taste of the past. A rich variety of natural beauty close by provides opportunities to explore caves, a waterfall, and secluded beaches. 34 rooms. Major credit cards.

Treasure Beach (South Coast)

Jake's $$-$$$ *Calabash Bay, Treasure Beach, St. Elizabeth, tel: 965-3145, 965-3185, 800-OUTPOST (toll-free from US and Canada); fax: 965-0552; e-mail: <reservations@islandoutpost.com>; website: <www.islandlife.com>.* An eclectic collection of colorful cottages set atop low cliffs in a secluded bay. Each room has a different theme, from Jamaican shack to Mexican pueblo. All have in-room CD players and free use of the hotel's extensive music collection. Tropical ceiling fans and mosquito nets maintain the traditional feel. Freshwater, rock-lined swimming pool; bar. 12 rooms. Major credit cards.

Sunset Resort Villas $$ *Calabash Bay, Treasure Beach, St. Elizabeth, tel: 965-0143, 800-786-8452 (toll-free from US); fax: 965-0555; website: <www.bizcom.com/sunsetresort>.* Set on landscaped gardens with native plants and trees, semiprivate beachfront, freshwater swimming pool, and large thatch canopies with swinging hammocks. All rooms have air-conditioning and ceiling fan. Large common living room available with satellite TV. Outdoor BBQ, poolside or indoor dining. 12 rooms. Major credit cards.

Kingston Area

Christar Villas $$$ *99-A Hope Road, Kingston 6, tel: 978-8066, 978-8071, 978-3933; fax: 978-8068.* Minutes away from the financial district of New Kingston and the Bob Marley Museum. Each room in this gated complex offers air conditioning, TV, telephone, and a fully equipped kitchenette. Swimming pool and fitness room. 22 rooms. Major credit cards.

Hotel Four Seasons $$-$$$ *18 Ruthven Road, Kingston 10, tel: 926-8805, 929-7655, 929-7657, 920-3547, 920-5552; fax: 929-5964; e-mail: <info@hotelfourseasonsja.com>; website: <www.hotelfourseasonsja.com>.* Converted from one of the city's fine Edwardian homes, the Four Seasons is less than five minutes' walk from New Kingston, behind secure walls in grounds embellished with a wide selection of tropical fruit trees. Fascinating combination of continental European and Jamaican styles. 76 rooms. Major credit cards.

Le Meridien Jamaica Pegasus $$$$ *81 Knutsford Boulevard, P.O. Box 333, Kingston 5, tel: 926-3690, 926-3699, 800-543-4300 (toll-free from US); fax: 968-4582; e-mail: <jmpegasus@toj.com>;website: <www.meridienjamaica.com>.* Situated in the financial and business district, close to many of the area's foremost attractions. All rooms are equipped with satellite TV, hair dryers, safes, electronic locks, complimentary coffee- and tea-making facilities, at least two telephones in the bedroom, and balconies with either mountain or pool/ocean view. Non-smoking floors. 350 rooms. Major credit cards.

Morgan's Harbour Hotel $$$$ *Port Royal, tel: 967-8030, 967-8040, 967-8060, 967-8075; fax: 967-8073; e-mail: <buccaneer@toj.com>.* Situated in Port Royal at the entrance to Kingston Harbour, with commanding views of the city skyline and the Blue Mountains. Spacious rooms with satellite TV; freshwater swimming pool, small private beach, complete scuba and water sports center. An acclaimed dining in the restaurant next to the yacht marina provides excellent evening views. 45 rooms. Major credit cards.

Strawberry Hill Hotel $$$$ *Irish Town, P.O. Box 590, St. Andrew's, tel. 944-8400, 800-OUTPOST (toll-free from US and Canada); fax: 944-8408; e-mail: <strawberryhill@islandoutpost.com>; website: <www.islandlife.com>.* All villas feature traditional 19th-century Jamaican architecture for an authentic Old World atmosphere. Near Kingston and surrounded by the Blue Mountains and extensive gardens, with exceptional panoramic views (including Kingston). In-room CD equipment with selection of music. 12 rooms. Major credit cards.

Recommended Restaurants

Jamaica offers a wide range of restaurants offering both local and international cuisine. Most of the larger resort hotels have acclaimed dining rooms that are open to the public. There are also many independent establishments with a high reputation and a faithful clientele. Unless otherwise indicated, all listed restaurants offer breakfast, lunch, and dinner daily.

Reservations are frequently necessary in the high season. In the off season, reservations are appreciated at all times but should definitely been made on weekends. Some of the more expensive establishments will have a dress code; you should inquire when you make your reservation. Many restaurants will offer free transport from and to your hotel when you make a booking. When calling from outside Jamaica, dial 876 before all telephone numbers listed below.

The following price categories indicate the approximate cost of a three-course meal, per person, excluding drinks; tips are extra. Prices are in US dollars:

$$$$$	over $80
$$$$	$50–$80
$$$	$30–$50
$$	$20–$30
$	under $20

Negril

Errol's Sunset Café $-$$ *Norman Manley Boulevard, Negril.* Located on the beach, this is an ideal place for lunch or a sunset drink. Excellent Jamaican meals, especially the selection of fresh soup, at very reasonable prices. It's not a place if you're in a rush, as all meals are cooked individually to ensure freshness. Cash only.

Gambino's $$$ *at The Beachcomber Club, Negril, tel: 957-4170.* Casually elegant dining outdoors with an ocean view. Usual

Jamaican favorites, along with authentic Italian food. Buffet and à la carte available. Free pick up service. Major credit cards.

Just Natural Restaurant $$ *West End Road, Negril.* Excellent vegetarian meals from appetizers to desserts, prepared to perfection with the addition of fresh fish daily. Major credit cards.

Kuyaba $$ *Norman Manley Boulevard, Negril, tel: 957-4318.* Caribbean and international cuisine set amid tropical foliage and Jamaican architecture. Full beach service during the day; happy hour from 4:30pm until the sun goes down. Free pick-up service. Major credit cards.

Margueritaville Bar and Grill $$-$$$ *Norman Manley Boulevard, Negril, tel: 957-4467.* Lively sports bar and grill located centrally on Negril's beach. Convenient for lounging on the beach, with full service available. Frequent "special" evenings with theme entertainment. Free pick-up service. Major credit cards.

Negril Tree House $$-$$$ *Norman Manley Boulevard, Negril, tel: 957-4287, 957-4288.* Jamaican food plus almost everything else, including pizzas, any time of day. Major credit cards.

The Pickled Parrot $$-$$$ *West End Road, Negril, tel: 957-4864.* A combination of Jamaican, American, and Mexican cuisine served in a cliff-top setting. Lounge chairs under thatched-roof huts, water chute into the sea, and rope swing provide extra entertainment. Free pick-up service. Major credit cards.

Rockhouse Restaurant and Bar $$$-$$$ *Rockhouse Hotel, West End Road, Negril, tel: 957-4373.* Serving Jamaican meals with European influences in a newly designed thatch-covered restaurant set on top of cliffs, providing an ideal location for sunset cocktails. Major credit cards.

Xtabi Cliff Restaurant $$-$$$ *Xtabi Resort, West End Road, Negril, tel: 957-4336.* Proud of their lobster and meat dishes chargrilled or cooked any other way. Cliff-top location overlooking the sea, about two miles out of town. Major credit cards.

Montego Bay

Marguerite's $$$$ *Gloucester Avenue, Montego Bay, tel: 952-4777.* Right on the waterfront; offers a more formal atmosphere and a great place to catch a sunset. Dinner only, morning until night. Major credit cards. (see Margueritaville, below, for the sports bar located in same establishment.)

Margueritaville $-$$ *Gloucester Avenue, Montego Bay, tel: 952-4777.* Lively sports bar and grill located at the start of the main strip in Montego Bay. Roof-top deck with water chute and floating trampoline. Frequent "special" evenings with theme entertainment. Free pick-up service. Major credit cards.

Tapas $$$ *Corniche Road, off Gloucester Avenue, Montego Bay, tel: 971-1921.* Elegant veranda dining on hillside above Gloucester Avenue. Music adds to the ambience and the stylish presentation of European cuisine with a touch of Jamaican flavoring. Dinner only, from morning until night. Major credit cards.

The Pork Pit $ *27 Gloucester Avenue, Montego Bay, tel: 940-3008, 971-5375.* Very basic but very good Jamaican food served through the kitchen window, with garden gazebos to sit and eat in. Cash only.

Walter's Bar and Grill $$ *39 Gloucester Avenue, Montego Bay, tel: 952-9391.* Casual dining in a sports-bar atmosphere. American and Jamaican cuisine, including buffalo wings (jerk-style) and burgers. This place is as popular with locals as it is with visitors, so it's a great place to meet people. Major credit cards.

Ocho Rios

The Little Pub $$-$$$ *59 Main Street, Ocho Rios, tel: 974-2324, 974-5825.* A center of cocktail bars and restaurants with live music six nights a week and the ubiquitous karaoke and large-screen satellite TV. A mixture of Jamaican specialities and American and European dishes in a lively setting. Major credit cards.

Port Antonio

Almond Tree $$$$ *in Hibiscus Lodge Hotel, Main Street, Ocho Rios; Tel. 974-2813.* A gourmet restaurant offering great views of the sea and serving international and local cuisine. Inside and open-air dining by candlelight. Major credit cards.

Blue Lagoon $$-$$$ *Fairey Hill, Port Antonio, tel: 993-7791/2, 993-7646.* Authentic Jamaican cuisine (including jerk chicken, pork, and fish), or choose your own lobster. A place with a spectacular setting. Lunch and dinner daily from 10am to 10pm. Live music most weekends. Major credit cards.

Evita's Italian Restaurant $$$$ *Eden Bower Road, Ocho Rios, tel: 974-2333, 974-1012, 974-1718.* Italian food with a touch of Jamaican spice. The essential place to see-and-be-seen, this is the only restaurant overlooking Ocho Rios and the sea. Everyone in the music, fashion, or film business has probably eaten here. Lunch and dinner daily from 11am–11pm. Major credit cards.

Mille Fleurs $$$ *in Hotel Mocking Bird Hill, Port Antonio, tel: 993-7267.* A creative mix of international and local cuisine that includes a good vegetarian selection. Most produce is locally grown, with some from the restaurant's own organic garden. Located in the foothills of the Blue Mountains with panoramic views. Dinner only, daily 7–10pm. Major credit cards.

Pavilion Restaurant $$$ *at Dragon Bay Beach Resort, Port Antonio, tel: 993-8751, 993-8753.* Overlooking the bay in a tranquil, casual setting, this spot offers a variety of international cuisine mixed with local specialities. Live entertainment each evening. Dinner only, daily 7–10pm. Major credit cards.

Trident Villas and Hotel $$$$$ *Port Antonio, tel: 993-2602.* Formal dining by candlelight with white-gloved waiters and antique furniture. Excellent food and service. Dinner only, daily 7–10pm. Major credit cards.

Treasure Beach (South Coast)

Jake's $$ *at Jake's resort, Calabash Bay, Treasure Beach, tel: 965-0110, 965-0114, 965-3146-8.* The best of Jamaica's spicy cuisine, including saltfish and ackee, rice and peas, fish in coconut milk, and Escovitch fish. The catch is always fresh. Soups include conch chowder, cream of pumpkin, red pea with pieces of beef and yam, and pepper pot. Major credit cards.

Yabba $$ *Treasure Beach Hotel, Treasure Beach, tel: 965-0110, 965-0114.* Jamaican and international food presented in a relaxed atmosphere. The owner grows many of the vegetables and fruits on his own farm. Major credit cards.

Kingston

Bullseye $$$ *Knutsford Boulevard, Kingston, tel: 960-8724, 960-8609, 960-8723.* Steaks to please the most discerning palates plus a great salad bar; this simple but straightforward combination is difficult to beat. Lunch and dinner daily, 10am–10pm. Major credit cards.

Jade Garden $$$ *106 Hope Road, Sovereign Center, Kingston, tel: 978-3476, 978-3479.* Hong Kong chefs prepare traditional Chinese food, and the island's two largest saltwater tanks ensure that all seafood is absolutely fresh. There is a choice of over 100 exotic dishes. Views of the Blue Mountains from picture windows are spectacular. Reservations recommended. Major credit cards.

Morgan's Harbour Hotel $$$ *Port Royal, tel: 967-8030.* Internationally acclaimed Jamaican and continental cuisine in a casual atmosphere overlooking Port Royal Marina, with views of the Kingston skyline across the bay. Major credit cards.

INDEX